Also by **Joseph L. Sax**

Water Law, Planning and Policy

Defending the
Environment

Defending the Environment

A Strategy for Citizen Action

Joseph L. Sax

Introduction by Senator George McGovern

ALFRED A. KNOPF   New York   1971

THIS IS A BORZOI BOOK
PUBLISHED BY ALFRED A. KNOPF, INC.

Library of Congress Catalog Card Number: 76-118718
Standard Book Number: 394-42351-8
Manufactured in the United States of America

Published February 3, 1971
Second Printing, February 1971
Third Printing, March 1971

Acknowledgments

To Gordon Harrison of the Ford Foundation, who encouraged my desire to write about law and the environment —before it became so popular a subject—I am deeply grateful. My work was done under a grant from the Ford Foundation. Resources for the Future, Incorporated, provided needed office space and supporting services for me during the year I spent in Washington. Dean Francis A. Allen of the University of Michigan Law School made it possible for me to take a leave of absence so that this book could be completed. My secretary, Lavinia Meddings, struggled with me through many drafts and mountains of paper; her help was indispensable.

I also acknowledge with thanks permissions from Yale University Press to reprint portions of my lecture "The Search for Environmental Quality: Role of the Courts," which appears in the book *Man's Struggle to Live with Himself: The Environmental Crisis,* edited by Harold W. Helfrich, Jr., 1970; from Ian McHarg to quote from *Design with Nature,* Natural History Press, 1969; from *The Christian Science Monitor* to quote from an article by George Favre on the Baltimore Expressway controversy, which appeared in the issue of February 6, 1970; from the *Wall Street Journal* to quote excerpts from a story by Alan L. Otten on the supersonic transport which appeared in the issue of November 12, 1969; and from William H. Tague to quote portions of his article "The Rise and Evaporation of the Mount Greylock Tramway," from the *Berkshire Review,* Vol. III, no. 1, Summer, 1967.

For Elli

"Plaintiffs refuse to accept the verdict of those best qualified to resolve such matters. . . . Congress has wisely left these technical matters to the technicians."

A Government lawyer seeking dismissal of citizen-initiated environmental lawsuits

"I have to say . . . that at the time we made the Santa Barbara decision there was no dissent in the Department. This was a sort of conservation 'Bay of Pigs,' you might say. . . ."

Former Secretary of the Interior Stewart L. Udall, testifying on the Santa Barbara oil spill

"Consumers are generally among the best vindicators of the public interest."

Warren E. Burger, Chief Justice of the United States

Introduction

The powerlessness of people to participate effectively in the institutional decisions that affect their lives marks the end of a true democratic society. In the United States today frustration abounds in nearly every area of human concern —the ending of a tragic war, the eradication of the silent violence of hunger, the extension of racial and human justice, and the reversing of an inexorable environmental tragedy which began two centuries ago.

In this remarkable book Professor Sax has touched on that mood of powerlessness, but has offered the alternatives of hope, vitality, and a brilliant proposal for tipping the balance of power toward the individual citizen in his efforts to save the environment.

In proposing that citizens be allowed to challenge industrial pollution and governmental inaction in the courts, Professor Sax observes that previous environmental legislation has created agencies rather than solutions and that agencies themselves often become the most serious obstacles to environmental preservation—not because of the malice of the administrators, but because of the complexities of the administrative process, the unique relationships between the regulators and the regulated, and, as Professor Sax quotes William Blake, "the mind-forged manacles" of law.

Among the "manacles of law" that have become the favored shibboleths of those who defend the actions of governmental agencies against challenge by individual citizens, perhaps the most anachronistic and pernicious is the doctrine of sovereign immunity, whose rationale—obviously erroneous—is that "the king can do no wrong."

Though the United States Supreme Court still holds to this doctrine, a most cogent statement about its implications was made by the Court in 1882:

> It seems to be opposed to all the principles upon which the rights of the citizen, when brought in collision with the acts of the government, must be determined. In such cases there is no safety for the citizen, except in the protection of the judicial tribunals, for rights which have been invaded by the officers of the government, professing to act in its name. There remains to him but the alternative of resistance, which may amount to crime.

Embodied in that statement of the Court are the two central theses of Professor Sax's book. The first is that the citizen does not need, and often cannot afford, a bureaucratic middleman to identify and prosecute his interest in environmental quality. Indeed, citizens working through groups such as the Environmental Defense Fund often find governmental agencies to be adversaries rather than colleagues. The second is that access to the courts of the United States is the most effective means for citizens to participate directly in environmental decisions and may be the only way to assure that democratic processes are brought to bear on environmental problems. Today, the access of citizens to the courts in environmental controversies is limited and often depends, as Professor Sax describes in Chapter 5, upon the existence of irrational factors wholly unrelated to the environmental controversy, such as, for example, the true definition of a "dike" or the "arbitrariness" of government officials.

In his proposal to permit a greater degree of citizen participation through the judicial system in resolving en-

vironmental problems, Professor Sax correctly observes
that the courts would not serve as a substitute for the legislative process, but as "a means of providing realistic access to
legislatures so that the theoretical processes of democracy
can be made to work more effectively in practice." The
judicial system traditionally has served as an institution for
heightening the public awareness of social problems, for
resolving controversies in an atmosphere free from unwarranted pressures, and for allowing citizens to participate in decisions which gravely affect their lives. By
removing the barriers to environmental litigation which
persist in the face of a national crisis, the courts become a
forum for citizen participation in democratic processes and
a catalyst for legislative action.

My concurrence with the theses which Professor Sax has
developed in this book is reflected in legislation that Senator Philip A. Hart of Michigan and I have introduced in
the United States Senate, and that Representative Morris
K. Udall of Arizona has introduced in the House of Representatives. This legislation embodies the principle of increased citizen participation through the courts that Professor Sax has proposed in his model statute. It is important
that the bills be enacted; regardless of their fate, however,
they are "an idea whose time has come," and for that we are
in great debt to Professor Sax.

GEORGE McGOVERN

Contents

Introduction   xi

Foreword   xvii

1. Fiasco at Hunting Creek   3

2. The Lesson of Hunting Creek   52

3. Why We Are Failing   63

4. A Role for the Courts   108

5. The Mind-Forged Manacles of Law   125

6. The Court as Catalyst   149

7. The Public Trust: A New Charter of
   Environmental Rights   158

8. Making Democracy Work: Remands
   to the Legislature   175

9. A Pause in Time: The Moratorium   193

10. Litigating Environmental Issues   212

11. Nice Sentiments Are Not Enough   231

Contents

Conclusion   240

Postscript   245

Appendix: A Model Law   247

Index   follows   page   252

Foreword

We are a peculiar people. Though committed to the idea of democracy, as private citizens we have withdrawn from the governmental process and sent in our place a surrogate to implement the public interest. This substitute—the administrative agency—stands between the people and those whose daily business is the devouring of natural environments for private gain.

The administrative agency is neither sinister nor superfluous; indeed, it is an essential institution to regulate the myriad daily activities which require that standards be set, permits granted, and routine rules enforced. But it has become more than merely a useful supplement to private initiatives and participation in the governmental process. It has supplanted the citizen as a participant to such an extent that its panoply of legal strictures actually forbid members of the public from participating even in the complacent process whereby the regulators and the regulated work out the destiny of our air, water, and land resources. The citizen who seeks to intervene in an administrative proceeding or to bring a complaint before the judiciary is shunted aside as a busybody or a crank, and a whole arsenal of legal weapons are wheeled out against him. The implementation of the public interest, he is told, must be left "to those who know best."

The long era which spawned and enforced those exclusionary rules is at last coming to an end. Members of the public have begun to see and smell and breathe the consequences of having relinquished initiative to professional regulators who, like mercenary soldiers, tend to develop a perspective of their own that is frequently at odds with the interest of their employers.

This is a book about the need to reassert citizen initiative in the management of our environment. It suggests that an essential format for reasserting participation in the governmental process is in the courtroom—not because judges are thought wiser or because the processes of litigation are particularly rapid, but because the court preeminently is a forum where the individual citizen or community group can obtain a hearing on equal terms with the highly organized and experienced interests that have learned so skillfully to manipulate legislative and administrative institutions. The court is attractive too because, free of the constraints which familiarity and close dealing tend to breed, it can bring fresh insights to problems of environmental management.

Courts are not to be used as substitutes for the legislative process—to usurp policies made by elected representatives —but as a means of providing realistic access to legislatures so that the theoretical processes of democracy can be made to work more effectively in practice. Citizen initiatives in the courts can be used to bring important matters to legislative attention, to force them upon the agendas of reluctant and busy representatives. To this end the judicially declared legislative remand and the court-ordered moratorium, now only shadowy ideas in the legal arena, must be refined and developed. This task is begun in the pages which follow.

Courts must also begin to put aside their traditional and unquestioning deference to administrative agencies; judges have too long lingered in the comfortable assumption that they could intervene only to challenge patent disregard of legislative rules, caprice, or corruption, ignoring the fact that a central problem of government lies in the vast area of administrative "discretion" that often masks submission to the demands of powerful interest groups.

The citizen, as a member of the public, must be recognized as having rights enforceable at law, equal in dignity and status to those of private property owners. The ancient notion of the public trust, of which every citizen is a beneficiary, must be revived and adapted to contemporary problems. Only then will concern with preservation of environmental quality truly be put on a footing with the interest in its exploitation.

If we are to save the environment, rather than merely revere it, the citizen can no longer be put off with the easy advice to "go get a statute enacted" or "wait until election day," while the bulldozer or chain saw stands ready to move.

No magic wand can be waved over the multitudinous problems of environmental quality. No elegant declaration of rights will simply and quickly solve our problems. Protracted struggle lies ahead, and the citizen fighting to vindicate his rights will be a central figure in that struggle. Regulation in the name of the public interest can no longer remain a two-party enterprise carried on between the regulated and the professional regulator. Effectuation of the public interest must begin to embrace the active participation of the public.

Defending the Environment

Chapter 1

Fiasco
at Hunting
Creek

No one paid any attention at the time, but the Alexandria, Virginia, *Gazette* for June 16, 1962, clearly signaled the trouble that was coming. The headline writers featured it as a legal dispute over a land auction; in retrospect, they would surely have written a very different story. A man named Vaughan Connelly had developed an apartment complex in Alexandria known as Hunting Towers, located on the shore of the Potomac River about halfway between Washington and Mount Vernon. The apartment houses were sold in 1958, but Connelly retained an adjacent 4.8-acre tract at the confluence of the Potomac and Hunting Creek. He had also borrowed $800,000 from the Teamsters Union pension fund, on which loan he defaulted, and thus the little tract at Hunting Creek, secured as collateral for the loan, went on the auction block.

The *Gazette* was intrigued with the legal intricacies involved—two bidders each claimed to have won the auction —and with the company which this Alexandria property was keeping: not only was Connelly in hock to the Teamsters and in bankruptcy himself, but the first mortgage on the property was held by a firm whose leading member was under indictment in Maryland. The paper noted only casually at the end of a long article that the "property is utilized as a parking lot, a sailing marina, and an unused swimming pool. Present zoning would permit construction of apartments on the land."

Ultimately the tract was sold to the Teamsters Union pension fund for more than $150,000 per acre. Of course people like to live on a river's edge with a view of the water, and urban shoreline property is always highly prized. But the astute observer might have noticed the special feature which gave these few acres unusual value— they commanded access to a much larger adjacent tract of shallowly submerged land. With a little dredging and filling, that small tract could be expanded into a much larger peninsula of land, all with a magnificent vista of the Potomac and the Washington skyline.

There were a few complications, to be sure, but nothing that would seem insuperable to a sophisticated developer. Because states ordinarily hold title to submerged shorelands in trust for the benefit of the public, it would be necessary to settle claims of public ownership. Filling in navigable waters also requires a permit from the U.S. Army Corps of Engineers. And while the area was scarcely of wilderness character, it did provide a nesting area for diving ducks and adjoined land managed by the National Park Service. Any proposed development would thus have conservation implications, but it was hardly the Grand Canyon or the Redwoods. Quiet diligence was called for.

The first step was taken October 9, 1963, when applications to fill 36.5 acres of submerged land adjacent to the 4.8-acre tract were filed with the Corps of Engineers by Hunting Towers Operating Company, owner of the existing apartment houses, and Howard P. Hoffman Associates, a New York real estate firm which held a contract to buy the 4.8-acre upland tract from the Teamsters pension fund.

Shortly after the applications for a landfill were filed, a state legislator from Alexandria, James Thomson, introduced a seemingly routine bill into the Virginia House of Delegates. It declared, with the usual "whereas-es," that the owners of the Hunting Creek tract claimed riparian rights and wished to fill the submerged land "so that productive use may be made thereof." It therefore authorized the Governor and Attorney General of Virginia to execute a deed to 36.5 acres—the same submerged land for which a fill permit had been filed with the Corps—conveying all the state's right, title, and interest for a sum to be fixed by the Governor, but not less than $60,000—about $1,600 per acre.

The bill was reported out of committee in four days. Two weeks later it passed the House unanimously on a day when one hundred bills were taken up. After another two weeks it was passed unanimously by the Senate on a day when sixty bills were before that body, and it became law only months thereafter. The bill engendered neither controversy nor debate as it made its way through the Virginia legislature. The document itself was not calculated to capture attention—beyond the brief statement of purpose mentioned above, its text was nothing more than a long legal description of the land in question, with the classic metes-and-bounds description of the "thence running south 2,707.33 feet" type.

To all appearances, it was a conventional piece of legislation settling a title uncertainty. While the bill was pending there was no public objection, which is hardly surprising since its existence seems to have eluded the attention of everyone but its proponents. Even upon its enactment, the law received no mention in the newspapers, and Delegate Thomson did not feel moved to issue a press release informing his constituents of his achievement. As the local paper put it many months later, the bill "was not mentioned in public statements by local legislators as among the activities of the session."

Because the bill involved their area, other local legislators had been routinely informed. Mrs. Marion Galland, who represented neighboring Arlington, was visited by the lawyer for Hunting Towers, whom she knew socially. He told her he was having Jim Thomson introduce the bill. "It's only a little old bill to use some wasteland," he said, "and it will bring increased tax revenues." Since he did not ask her to sponsor the legislation and because she was not aware of any objections to it, she made no further inquiries.

It was not until some months later that Mrs. Galland began to hear from friends in Alexandria that the law had significant conservation implications. As opposition became more vocal, she publicly announced that she would have voted against the bill had she known at the time the information which was later brought to her attention.

Was she saying that a bill which was essentially the reflection of a single delegate's desires could become a duly enacted law of the state? "In a two-month period, we have before us fifteen hundred bills," she said. "Nobody is going to know enough to raise the red flag unless it's called to attention." But while the bill was pending no one outside the legislature even seemed to be aware of its existence. Where is the initiative to begin? "That is precisely the point," Mrs. Galland replied. "Citizen groups do not get alarmed in time, and developers are smart enough to associate themselves with the ruling caste in the legislature. The power structure in the legislature is allied with business interests."

Between March 1964, when the bill was signed into law,[1] and the summer of that year, public opposition first began to mobilize. It was still not too late, for Governor Albertis S. Harrison had not signed the deed to the land. In July, there was every reason for the developers to remain confident. On the thirtieth, the Alexandria *Gazette* carried the headline, "Animal Welfare League Attempts to Stop Land Fill." The League had written the Governor and Secretary of the Interior Stewart L. Udall, noting that while its interests might seem remote from a landfill proposal,

> . . . we had become acutely aware of the dislocation of wildlife. We have had to rescue some 400 opossums and assorted other birds and reptiles that had been forced into the city. We can only speculate as to how many others have starved or been killed off in the competition for survival in their dwindling habitat. We cite this experience to indicate our very real interest in saving the natural areas that remain around Alexandria.

With the mild-mannered Animal Welfare League as their only vocal opponents, the developers did not yet have much to worry about. Joel T. Broyhill, U.S. Representative from Arlington, had also received a letter from the League and announced that he was keeping the matter "under serious consideration." His legislative assistant said Broy-

---

[1] Ch. 546 of the Acts of Assembly of Virginia (March 31, 1964).

7

hill was "watching it very carefully." Enter and exit Mr. Broyhill.

Meanwhile, Mrs. Galland, who had been asked to prevail upon the Governor not to sign the deed, failed to do so. She fully intended to, as she recalled five years later, but went off to Europe with her husband that summer and simply forgot all about it. In any event, Mrs. Galland noted, her representations would hardly have been likely to be effective, which was what she had meant about developers associating themselves with the "ruling caste in the legislature." For Jim Thomson, the bill's sponsor, was a powerful member of the House leadership and was related by marriage to the Byrd family, epitome of the Establishment in American political life. The Governor would have been unlikely to be ready to go out on a limb for some bird watchers whose cause was being advanced by a junior delegate from Northern Virginia.

Mrs. Galland was only speculating, however astutely. But several years later another Northern Virginia legislator found out precisely how right she was. Delegate Clive DuVal of McLean had also been asked to intervene; he wrote the Governor and asked him to withhold action on the deed. The Governor was "studying the matter"; six years after the bill became law, it was still being studied.

As of the summer of 1964, the emerging landfill controversy was in suspended disarray. Enough had happened to indicate a degree of local opposition, but the opponents seemed to have nowhere to go. The legislature was out of session; the Governor's position was uncertain, and there was no basis for confidence that he would not sign the deed rather soon after the matter was dropped by the newspapers. The Animal Welfare League, local opponents of high-rise buildings, and scattered conservationists were not mobilized for decisive action. The bulldozers might soon have been at work if attention had not shifted suddenly and surprisingly to the federal scene.

The fill permit was still pending before the Corps of Engineers. As is customary in such matters, the Corps referred the application for comment to the Bureau of Sport Fisheries and Wildlife of the U.S. Department of the Interior. The inquiry went to the regional office in Atlanta, where, as is also customary, it received what is known as a "desk review"—that is, officials looked over the documents and without further investigation decided that the matter was not worthy of a field investigation in light of their limited staff and other pressing business. Ordinarily in such circumstances, the application would have been returned to the Corps without comment—giving neither Interior's approval or disapproval.

In Washington, however, the Bureau decided that a study should be made. "The reason that this was done," Dr. John S. Gottschalk, the Director of the Bureau, later explained, "was because at this time, back in 1963 and 1964, there was an awakening of interest in trying to do something about improving the character and condition of the Potomac River." The regional office was ordered to make a study and report, and they determined to oppose the permit. The Corps was so informed in March 1964; in June, at the Corps' request, a detailed statement of opposition, with supporting data, was prepared by the Fish and Wildlife Service.

At this time, while rudimentary efforts were still being made at the state level to keep the deed from issuing, the

9

project's opponents apparently were unaware of the strong dissent that had been entered by the Interior Department and was sitting in the Corps' files. Probably the report would ultimately have been brought to public attention, but no effort was then made to publicize it either by the Corps or the Interior Department. Local opponents and federal officials each went their own ways. Indeed, as late as August of that year, months after the negative study by the Fish and Wildlife Service had been filed, the local paper reported only that Secretary of the Interior Udall "is believed to be interested in preserving Dykes Marsh," an adjacent area. It was not until December—when the project had already been shelved—that a report appeared in the paper stating, without elaboration, that the landfill application was opposed by the Fish and Wildlife Service.

Sometime during the summer of 1964, again quite independently from the activities of local opponents, three U.S. Congressmen became interested in the landfill application and protested against it to both the Corps and the Department of the Interior. The three—Representatives Henry S. Reuss of Wisconsin, John P. Saylor of Pennsylvania, and John E. Moss of California—were all staunch conservationists, though it has never been clear why they undertook to intervene in this particular matter, which at the time seemed only one of thousands of local conservation controversies. Apparently they were not acting at the request of local citizens. Perhaps the presence of a controversy over the Potomac, almost literally in the shadow of the Capitol, attracted their attention, as it did that of the Fish and Wildlife Service. Some observers think it relevant that Representative Moss resided and owned land in the affected area of Alexandria.

In any event, by the autumn of 1964 a combination of opposition forces had coalesced sufficiently to halt the project. With an adverse technical report from its staff and protests by several Congressmen, the Interior Department was obviously going to stand in opposition; local opposition was sufficiently overt—if not independently powerful—to assure that denial of the permit would not be viewed as an affront to a united Alexandria community. In December the Corps wrote the applicants that it would take no further action to approve the requested permits. Interestingly, the Corps did not deny the permits nor did the proponents withdraw their applications. The proposal was simply shelved. Experienced opponents might have sensed that the time was ripe to move in for the kill—to seek a decisive rejection of the permit. But the Animal Welfare League and its allies do not have an institutional instinct for the jugular. The battle appeared to be won, and no one seemed inclined to disturb that rare event—a conservation victory achieved with relative ease.

Of course the developers had barely begun to fight, but they did not favor open combat. For three full years the Hunting Creek landfill dropped from public attention. When the dispute got back into the headlines much later, the Alexandria *Gazette* published an editorial entitled "Landfill Lull" and quoted a local speculator who, upon being denied a rezoning permit in another matter, had remarked philosophically: "Money can always wait." It should be inscribed on a plaque at Hunting Creek.

While the conservationists went back to saving possums, the developers hired themselves a law firm in which one of the principal partners was the nephew of John W. McCormack, Speaker of the U.S. House of Representatives.

There is no evidence that Speaker McCormack himself ever became involved in the Hunting Creek matter, but perhaps there is, after all, something in a name. Mystery shrouds the activities of the developers and their law firm between December 1964, when the landfill application was inactivated, and October 10, 1967. But then the most extraordinary thing happened.

Out of the blue, the Assistant Secretary of the Interior for Fish and Wildlife, Dr. Stanley A. Cain, sent a letter to the Corps of Engineers, noting Interior's previous opposition to the Hunting Creek landfill and then continuing:

> However, since that time we have reconsidered our interests in this matter. In the light of existing conditions in the area, we have concluded that the granting of the applications would not significantly affect recreation or conservation values in the Hunting Creek area. Accordingly, we withdraw the objections interposed to the granting of the permits in accordance with the revised applications.

In the three-year period preceding Cain's letter, the developers had reduced the acreage sought to be filled, in response to concerns about Alexandria's sewage disposal and the riparian rights asserted by the National Park Service for their adjacent land at Jones Point; however, even with those changes the Park Service and the Bureau of Sport Fisheries and Wildlife maintained their objections to the fill. In fact, Cain's statement in his letter that "we have reconsidered our interests in this matter" was supported neither by new field studies nor by revised evaluations on the part of expert staff members.

Indeed, Cain had not even notified the Director of the Bureau of Sport Fisheries and Wildlife, Dr. Gottschalk, that the letter had been sent, though Gottschalk was the official upon whose staff reports the Interior Department's opposition to the permit had been based. More significantly, as it turned out, Cain failed to notify those Congressmen who had earlier expressed opposition to the landfill. The various responses of concerned officials and agencies to Cain's unusual course of action is most instructive.

The first one to learn about the letter was Gottschalk, who at all times during this extended controversy remained firm in his opposition. Nonetheless, when Gottschalk was interviewed in 1969 he described his reaction this way:

> Someone in the Department called to tell me about the letter that Stan Cain had sent, withdrawing opposition to the permit, and I went charging over to see Cain. I said to him, "Do you realize what you have done? You have fixed it so that we can't help you even if you really want to do this, and I don't think you do." Cain replied that he understood this withdrawal of opposition is what the Secretary wants, that Representative John Dingell [of Michigan], chairman of the important Subcommittee on Fisheries and Wildlife Conservation, had withdrawn his opposition, and that, as he understood it, the value of the area was not great.

What had Gottschalk meant about Cain fixing it so that Gottschalk could not help him? He replied that "Cain had been nudged" and that he would have been willing "to try to protect Stan against getting a bloody nose because of the response likely to arise from members of

Congress opposed to the project when they found out that Interior had withdrawn its opposition."

When asked how he could have protected Cain, Gottschalk said that "Stan could have twisted my arm, maybe" —that the Fish and Wildlife Service might have reconsidered their technical investigation and have provided a report upon which objections could be withdrawn. "But," he observed, "Cain said, 'I'll take the political heat for this; that's what I'm paid for.' "

Gottschalk did not know and said he did not want to know the source of the "political heat" that had "nudged" Cain. These comments by him followed a rather extended monologue in which he strongly affirmed his feeling that to have permitted the landfill would have been a grave error—"a terrible opening wedge," as he described it, "the key to opening the door to destruction of the Potomac."

One is rarely privileged to see the interplay between personal relations and policy-making so clearly displayed. Certainly Cain and Gottschalk had mutual respect. Had Cain come to Gottschalk before the letter was sent, he would undoubtedly have been treated to a vigorous argument against the landfill permit. But Cain was considerate enough not to want to involve his colleague in the intricacies of weighing political and professional judgments against each other. Once the letter had been sent, and the damage done, Gottschalk's first thought was for the impact on his associate, a skilled professional, naïvely trapped in a politically untenable situation.

It did not take long for Assistant Secretary Cain to find out just how badly trapped he was. On November 16, 1967, Representative Moss wrote Cain to find out if it were true that the Department had withdrawn its opposition;

Cain replied with a letter that plunged him even deeper into the dilemma:

> This responds to your letter of November 16. . . . While it is true that this Department interposed objections to both the original applications and the revised applications, the conservation values which would have been affected were relatively minimal. I understand that objections on conservation grounds were filed, nevertheless, in support of opposition to the proposed development from other governmental sources. However, much of the opposition has been withdrawn and it seems to us to be the sensible course of action to withdraw our objection . . . since it was made primarily in support of those who, in part at least, have now changed their minds.

Like a good cross-examiner, Moss played his cards out slowly, letting the witness build obstacles he would have then to pass.

> I assume [Moss wrote] the original action of opposition was based on careful studies of the effect upon wildlife. . . . If my initial premise is correct, then certainly there must be some sort of study upon which you based your subsequent action. Or is it your intention to tell me that you made a "judgment" without any additional studies by the experts of the Fish and Wildlife Service?

Of course Moss knew the answer, and he got what he wanted—a letter from Cain stating: "I can tell you that I did make a judgment without any additional studies of the fish and wildlife values at the site."

Finally there was the Corps of Engineers. Being in receipt of Cain's letter, it blandly informed Representative Reuss that the Corps was considering the issuance of the permit. Thus matters stood at the end of 1967. At the state level, things were quiescent; state officials were no doubt glad to have responsibility for an increasingly divisive issue shifting to the federal government. The Governor of Virginia still had not issued the deed, and the question was still being studied in his office. Local opposition was very quiet and apparently unaware of the heat being generated among federal agencies; the newspapers carried no Hunting Creek news between December 1964 and December 1967.

Strategically, it was not clear in December where the center of gravity of the controversy lay. Interior had locked itself into an uncomfortable posture, but thus far it was an unpublicized discomfort. Congressional opposition was strong but very limited; congressional advocates of the project—if there were any—were being very reticent. Representative Dingell's name had not been mentioned openly, though obviously it was his changed attitude—quietly withdrawing earlier quiet opposition—to which Cain had referred in his letter to Moss. The Corps was seemingly indifferent and probably wanted to get the matter resolved with as little noise as possible, whichever way it was to go. Its strategy was self-protective, as it usually is in the implementation of its dredge-and-fill permit function. Aware of significant differences of opinion about the project, however, the Corps decided to hold a public hearing.

By mid-December it became obvious that Interior was not going to back down. Representatives Moss and Reuss held a meeting on December 12 at which Cain was asked to appear; he sent an assistant in his place. In the world of Washington symbolism, that seemed an important clue. If there were still any doubts, they were resolved in January when Cain informed the Corps that Interior would not testify at the forthcoming Corps hearings.

Plainly something had to be done if the process was not now to move along inexorably toward a grant of the permit. It was time for the technique of the "new revelations, new dimensions to the controversy." On December 16, 1967, Hunting Creek hit the newspapers again with the headline "Apartment Foes Cite Race Issue." Moss and Reuss were charging that Hunting Towers, one of the applicants, was a notorious practitioner of racial discrimination, and they sought to bring the Corps of Engineers directly into the issue by asking the Secretary of the Army, Stanley R. Resor, to reject the landfill application on the ground that it would serve a segregated apartment project, and particularly one that discriminated against Negro servicemen.

It was a nice ploy, but it was not enough. Somewhere along the line, the Hunting Towers Operating Company withdrew its application from active consideration, and the permit had been reduced to a request for 9.5 acres of fill sought solely by Howard P. Hoffman Associates. This might have been the time for a careful investigation into the underlying ownership of the various interests involved, which were at best confused and complex. It might not only have cast some light on the mysterious change of position by Stanley Cain at the Interior Department, but also could conceivably have been used to illuminate the controversy's relation to the Byzantine world of real estate development.

The economic interests in the land were tantalizingly

vague. Howard P. Hoffman owned a contract to purchase the Hunting Creek tract (for which the permit was being sought) from the Teamsters pension fund. While Hoffman refused to reveal the terms of the contract, it would presumably have been economically advantageous to the pension fund if the permit were granted, since Hoffman's purchase from the Teamsters was apparently conditional upon obtaining permission to fill. Hoffman also said that he alone, with some minor interest held by members of his family, was the sole owner of the right to purchase the land from the pension fund. Yet at the Corps hearing in 1968 a man named John Schwartz, of Columbus, Ohio, testified that he was part of Hoffman Associates and said: "I own an important part of the land under question here." Hoffman, however, denied that Schwartz owned any interest in the proposed development at Hunting Creek. Schwartz remains a mystery, except, as we shall see, that it was he who indirectly brought Senator Birch Bayh of Indiana into the Hunting Creek morass.

Hunting Towers itself was sold in 1958 to a group of investors, who themselves sold the apartments in 1964 to people whom the firm handling the transaction would describe only as a group composed of "very well-known men from New York." When interviewed in 1969, Hoffman's lawyer, Sanford Grossman, said that one of the owners of Hunting Towers was former Governor Thomas E. Dewey of New York. Upon receiving notes of that interview for confirmation, Grossman replied: "You have quoted me as making an affirmative statement of fact about Mr. Dewey, for which I would have no basis. I believe that in response to your query it might be said that: 'We have heard names like Mr. Dewey associated with this property.' "

Whether the landfill in question is consistent with intelligent planning for the Potomac River Basin ought not to depend on who wants it filled—not, that is, unless the government agencies charged with worrying about the Potomac worry themselves about who wants it filled. The staff counsel for the congressional subcommittee which ultimately held hearings on Hunting Creek was asked whether his investigations had revealed the identity of the investors. They had not, he said, because he had not been asked to discover this information by the Congressmen involved. He seemed slightly miffed at the suggestion that a study of Hunting Creek should have been turned in this direction; the issue, he said, involves resource policy—whether we are going to let the Potomac be nibbled away by such developments—and not political influence.

The Corps hearing on February 21, 1968, was something of an anticlimax. The proponents of the landfill explained their project, resting their case essentially on the ground that the area in question was already seriously degraded, an assertion which no one ever questioned. Representative Reuss spoke at length in opposition, reiterating that the technical objections of the Interior Department had never been rebutted, that the racial discrimination problem should be considered, and that the project should not be approved so long as Hunting Towers practiced discrimination even though its owners were no longer formally associated with the application.

Local citizen groups asserted that despite its present condition, the area retained important wildlife values, and—more significantly—that the way to deal with past mistakes in development was not to repeat them but to correct them with restoration of the Potomac estuary.

Perhaps the most notable aspect of the hearing was the absence of state and local government agencies. The Governor of Virginia, still studying away, sent no representative either from his office or from any other state agency such as the Game and Fisheries Commission. No state legislators or county officials appeared, and a representative of the City of Alexandria testified that the City was concerned only with the engineering aspects of sewage disposal and that it "has taken no position with respect to the esthetic or conservation aspects of the proposal."

And, of course, there was no representative of the Department of the Interior, the only agency whose personnel had studied the landfill proposal. Although "the concerned Bureaus usually do appear and testify at Corps of Engineer hearings," Assistant Secretary Cain had decided that "this is an exceptional case in which . . . we decided there was no need to appear." It would seem that the most "exceptional" thing about the case was the fact that Cain's withdrawal of Interior Department objections had been made without the knowledge or agreement of the Bureaus involved.

What happened next—between the time of the Corps hearing in February and its action on the application in May 1968—involved one of those fortuities which seem endemic to the governmental process. Mike Frome, a well-known outdoors writer and conservation editor of *Field and Stream* magazine, who lived near Mount Vernon, became involved in the case. According to Frome,

I found myself one day enjoying the most delightful

daydream, in which I was privileged to spend my career writing about the natural and intellectual glory of America . . . and then the telephone rang. . . . It was a little old lady in tennis shoes. I could tell by the tone in her voice . . . "I have read your article in *Southern Living* about the Everglades," said she, "but you do not fully impress me. It is one thing to advocate protection of endangered birds a thousand miles away, but why have you been silent about endangered birds at Hunting Creek on the Potomac River, close to your home? . . ." The lady left me no alternative but to pursue the issue.

Frome began to make inquiries, and Cain began to get worried; Dr. Gottschalk's predictions of the previous October were beginning to come to pass. Uncomfortable as his relations with Reuss and Moss were already, they were at least quiet thus far, limited to abrasive letters sitting in congressional and Interior Department files. But the anticipation of publicity from a noted conservation writer would be most unpleasant. Cain at last began to realize just how unprotected he was in having withdrawn objections to the permit without any support from his experts.

On March 15, 1968, Cain sent the following formal memorandum to the Bureau of Sport Fisheries and Wildlife:

> The pot still boils on the decision I made some time ago to remove objections to this permit. . . . The latest difficulty arises from Mike Frome who has asked that I reverse myself. . . . Today I had a chance to speak to Secretary Udall about the problem. He had earlier relegated the decision to me and had raised no objection to what I did. He merely wishes that we get a scientific-

technical basis that can be stood on, whether we go "yes" or "no" on issuance of the permit. . . . Whatever the judgment of the Bureau turns out to be, I will go with it, as will the Secretary. Incidentally, I will not be bothered by reversing myself, if it will turn out that way. And if it doesn't, I'll have to take Mike Frome's possible barbs. *C'est la guerre!*

On April 4 George B. Hartzog, Jr., Director of the National Park Service, replied:

An important principle; that is, the preservation of our fast-disappearing environment . . . would appear to me to be involved here. The bills before Congress to preserve estuarine areas, and the Potomac River study as well, highlight the need to preserve the natural environment along the Potomac estuary. . . . The alteration of wetland areas . . . where they are at a premium . . . could set a precedent which might have disastrous consequences along the Potomac estuary and elsewhere. In short, this small concession at Hunting Creek might be pointed to as a precedent for the right to undertake far larger and more destructive high-rise projects in other embayments along the Potomac. All things considered, I recommend the desirability of the Department restudying its recent decision at Hunting Creek [i.e., the decision to withdraw opposition to the proposed landfill].

On April 8 Cain responded to the Park Service with a memorandum that, though probably written to be self-serving, was to be much regretted by Cain when Representative Reuss got hold of it:

. . . I would like to clarify my role, which has not been an enviable one. I was told . . . that the original field report . . . was in weak opposition to the permit and that the fish and wildlife values claimed for the area were "upgraded" here in Washington . . . that this was at least partly in response to certain congressional opinions . . . before I was Assistant Secretary. When the matter was brought to my attention . . . I was informed that some of the congressional objections had been withdrawn. John Dingell had done so in writing. . . . It was implified that others were no longer opposed. *It was at that point that I withdrew Interior's opposition, a decision based first on political considerations* and second on the feeling that the values were not great in the area to be filled. . . . I will be happy to reverse myself if [Fish and Wildlife] makes a strong case and if [the National Park Service] can give me evidence of the important values. [Italics added.]

The next day, April 9, Dr. Gottschalk sent Cain a strong memorandum in opposition to the landfill, concluding: "I think we must urge the Corps not to grant this permit." On April 10 Cain wrote Gottschalk: "I am in the position of having to accept your statements of the . . . values associated with the site . . . and I do so gladly. What this means is that I am now reversing the position that I took earlier." That same day Cain called the Corps to tell them that he had reversed himself.

Cain did not act a moment too soon, for the Corps was about to issue the permit. At this point the Corps decided to refer the matter to the Under Secretary of the Interior for his formal decision as to the position of the

Department. Why exactly the Corps did this, rather than simply accepting Cain's reversal of position as a reinstatement of objection to the permit, has been a matter of some dispute.

There was in effect a memorandum of understanding between the Corps and Interior requiring that "unresolved substantive differences" on landfill permits be referred to the Under Secretary of the Interior. Whether there were unresolved differences is not clear. The Corps had never taken the position that it wanted to issue the permit even if Interior opposed it, and, indeed, earlier they had taken just the opposite position. That is, they had refused to issue a permit so long as Interior opposed it. Nor, as of April 10, were there differences within Interior—everyone there at that point agreed in opposing the permit.

But the precise meaning of the memorandum of understanding is irrelevant. The point is simply that, as of April 10, the Corps seemed to have a choice—it could have accepted Cain's current opposition as the position of Interior and gone on from there or, as it did, have referred the matter back to Interior for another view by a more highly placed official. As it turned out, it made a difference; the Under Secretary, David S. Black, reversed Cain's reversal of Cain's earlier reversal of departmental objections. By late April 1968, Interior was back to its earlier "no objection" position, and the next month the Corps granted the permit.

If the attempt to keep Interior's formal positions straight seems confusing, it is not nearly as confusing as the underlying facts. Why had Cain undergone this change of mind between October 1967 and April 1968? One version, taken from departmental memos, has already been described: Cain, under pressure from prospective bad publicity, felt impelled to take a new position which was supported by the evidence, the theory being that at best he could support that position with expert views and at worst would have to reverse himself again. But he would at least have a present position which could not be criticized. He got the evidence, reversed himself on that basis, and accepted the professional judgment of his staff "gladly," if with some embarrassment.

Dr. Gottschalk tells essentially the same story but in a version which makes Cain look rather better. The story begins the same way but ends with Cain coming into Gottschalk's office and saying:

> John, I've been thinking about Hunting Creek and I decided that I was wrong in changing my mind, and I'm going to change it back and reinstate my opposition. A lot of people have been talking to me, and I've decided that I had bad advice when I signed that letter last October. If I made a mistake, I want to correct it.

Oddly enough, Cain explained his April reversal in terms that are far less flattering to himself. In July Cain, under questioning from Representative Guy Vander Jagt of Michigan, told a congressional subcommittee that it was his present position, as of July 1968, that Interior should not have objected to the landfill. He was taking the position that Interior should *not* have opposed the granting of the permit, that he had been right in October 1967 and wrong in April 1968 when he reinstated opposition. How then, he was asked, did he come to reinstate his objections in April?

Here is his testimony, taken directly out of the printed congressional hearings:[2]

DR. CAIN: I also explained that by saying that a good deal of impact had come on me in the interim [between October 1967 and April 1968] from one source or another. And I called together my personal staff . . . and my flip-flop—and there is only one—is that I was advised by them unanimously to change my position, because if I did not I would have trouble.

MR. VANDER JAGT: And did you?

DR. CAIN: Yes, I changed it. Because I had the unanimous advice of my staff to do so.

MR. VANDER JAGT: And now you are changing that position?

DR. CAIN: But I have also told you that my personal opinion, taking everything into consideration, today is the same as it was on October 10.

MR. VANDER JAGT: So your reversal of your reversal you do not agree with any more. In your personal opinion, you just did that because your staff told you to do it?

DR. CAIN: That is right. That is what I have said. I followed my staff—

. . .

MR. VANDER JAGT: So when you reversed the reversal you did not agree with that action that you took; is that correct?

DR. CAIN: I think I agreed with advice that this was probably in a tactical sense to my advantage. . . . I explained

2 "Permit for Landfill in Hunting Creek, Virginia." Hearings before the Subcommittee on Natural Resources and Power, Committee on Government Operations, House of Representatives, 90th Cong., 2nd Sess. (1968); *id.,* part 2 (1969).

that that reversal, if you please, was made on the unanimous advice of my staff for nonscientific, nontechnical
reasons.

This extraordinary admission will seem peculiar only
to one who fails to sense the rhythm and nuance of the governmental process. It must be remembered that this
testimony, given in July, came while the official Interior
Department position—determined by the Under Secretary
—was one of no opposition to the permit. Thus Cain's
testimony, self-deprecatory as it was, put him in agreement
with his superior, the Under Secretary, and in accord with
the Corps, which by then had granted the permit largely on
the basis of the Under Secretary's "no objection" position.

As of mid-April 1968, the matter was in the hands of
Under Secretary Black, whose role has been a matter of
some controversy. A number of people—including the
congressional investigators—seem to think that the question was referred to him by the Corps because it could
be anticipated that he would take a politically acceptable
position of "no objection" that Cain was at that point
either unwilling or unable to take.

Whatever Black's motivation, and however much or
little he was attuned to the politics of the landfill, the
significance of his intervention has quite a different point.
For Black overtly rejected both the technical staff studies
recommending opposition and the professional judgment
of people like Gottschalk. Whatever Black's views were
about conservation, the point is that he was a lawyer and
that his judgment about Hunting Creek represented a
legal analysis of the Interior Department's role in the case.
As he himself later explained,

I have the deepest respect for the scientific and technical capability of the Department's staff. I seek and value their advice. I yield to it on technical matters and am influenced by it on policy issues. In my view, however, the views expressed by some of those staff members in this instance represented subjective value judgments or preferences not based on clearly demonstrable evidence . . . to interfere with the use of private property to the extent of preventing its development requires some basis in law, supported by convincing proof that public values are threatened. . . . The record . . . persuaded me that a return to the departmental position of blanket opposition to the permit would constitute arbitrary and capricious action.

One can be perplexed by Black's analysis on a number of grounds. His law itself is odd, to say the least, for it is hardly clear that an application to fill navigable waters (which is the basis for Corps jurisdiction over the application) is a "use of private property." Even if he were correct, however, it seems clear that the matter was not referred to Interior for a legal decision on that question. Since the Corps is the permit-granting agency, presumably *it* is to make the decision whether the evidence presented is legally sufficient to support the conclusions sought to be drawn from that evidence. The statute under which such permits are referred by the Corps to Interior makes this quite explicit. It provides that the Corps

shall consult with the United States Fish and Wildlife Service . . . [to obtain] the reports and recommendations of the Secretary of the Interior . . . *based on* surveys and investigations conducted by the United States Fish and

Wildlife Service . . . for the purpose of determining the possible damage to wildlife resources and for the purpose of determining means and measures that should be adopted to prevent the loss or damage to such wildlife resources. . . . [Italics added.]

These things are not noted in order to explicate the law relating to dredge-and-fill permits, but rather to indicate the extraordinary change of role which occurred with Black's intervention. If the permit decision on a matter like Hunting Creek were someday to come before a court, for example, the conventional judicial response would be a refusal to look behind the decision on the ground that it is not the function of the courts to second-guess technical experts in the area of their special expertise.

This may be perfectly sensible if in fact the decision were the decision of aquatic biologists about impacts on fish and wildlife. But in the Hunting Creek case, the decision reflected in the Interior Department's position as determined by Under Secretary Black—himself a lawyer —was simply a legal determination that (1) private property was at stake, (2) that Interior was not authorized to oppose the filling of that property in the absence of "convincing proof that public values are threatened," and (3) that the record contained no such convincing proof.

It is rather an intricate game that is played here. When an official like Black is brought before a congressional investigating committee and asked why he overruled his technical experts, he explains that he made a determination of law that their conclusions were not supported by the evidence. But had Interior been brought into a court, it is predictable that the Department's lawyers would have defended the decision as a matter of expert discretion which judges are neither competent nor authorized to probe.

One would have to search very diligently to find a government department saying, in any lawsuit where its technical experts were under challenge, what Under Secretary Black said at the hearings in explaining why he had departed from the advice of those experts. Staff experts, he indicated, were really concerned about a bad precedent and not about the values of this particular area, though they had sought to identify values at Hunting Creek. As to this, Black said,

> . . . we can take our stand on legitimate grounds and support them on the basis of real conservation values, not makeweight arguments and statistical manipulations. . . .

. . .

MR. MOSS: Are you charging that your Bureau of Sport Fisheries engaged in statistical manipulations?

MR. BLACK: I think that statistics can be very misleading. And I think it can be demonstrated at this point that they are.

MR. MOSS: That isn't what you said. You said statistical manipulation. I regard that as a charge that your subordinate agencies have engaged in that practice. Is that what you want this record to reflect?

MR. BLACK: Our subordinate agencies are very vigorous in protecting the interests that they deem within their particular parameter.

MR. MOSS: Is it your allegation that they have engaged in statistical manipulation?

MR. BLACK: That was my testimony.

MR. MOSS: All right. I just wanted it to be clear.

This brings us back to the Corps of Engineers. As of early April 1968, it was waiting to make its decision. Presumably one important element it was to consider was the evidence brought out in the February hearing. At that time, however, the public knew nothing about the internal machinations at Interior; in February Cain had not yet repented of his opposition, whether for scientific or tactical reasons. It was only known that the official departmental position was one of no opposition. Despite all the changes in the interim, the Corps did not decide to hold a second hearing. And when the Corps finally received Black's letter of April 26 reinstating or affirming a "no objection" position by Interior, it is not at all clear how it was to evaluate that letter—whether it was to be treated as a legal statement, a policy position about development of the Potomac, a judgment about the politics of the case, or an evaluation of the technical data available. Black's letter to the Corps hardly made things clear. The critical paragraph said:

> As to the damage to conservation values, I have received and considered the views of people in and out of this Department. . . . I have also made a visual inspection of the affected area. . . . While there is no doubt of the opinions reached by those concerned with the conservation impact, their position is founded on subjective judgment considerations rather than any factual evidence which would support valid objections by this Department.

The Corps was at this point in what Cain had elsewhere described as "an unenviable position." No one but the Interior Department had actually studied the area, and it had no objection to the permit. Nonetheless it was obvious that Interior was not following the advice of its own experts. The City of Alexandria was unwilling to take a position on anything but sewage disposal. The County had made no appearance. The Virginia Commission of Game and Fisheries was of the view that since the legislature had passed a statute authorizing conveyance of the land in 1964, the matter of possible effects of a landfill on waterfowl or other wildlife resources of the state had already been decided by legislative action.

The Corps might have set out to make its own investigation; things were certainly tangled enough at Interior to suggest the usefulness of a fresh viewpoint. But that would have been for the Corps to thrust itself into the middle of what was at best an uncomfortably controversial matter in which a lot of people would be dissatisfied with either outcome. The prudent thing was to be deferential; if Interior—the principal government agency with expertise on the matter—could find no basis for objection, the safe course was to issue the permit and let Interior take responsibility, even though everyone knew that Interior's expertise had not been determinative of the Department's position.

Far from being over on May 29, 1968, when the Corps issued the permit, the Hunting Creek controversy had barely begun. The wrath of a Congressman frustrated is something to reckon with, and Henry Reuss had reason to be more than a little annoyed. He had fought hard and long, had made his interest very clear, and been treated rather cavalierly by Interior—they had not bothered to keep him informed of various developments as they occurred, and even when he and Representative Moss had made specific inquiries, they had been met with that very special kind of vague response which governmental officials usually reserve for obscure citizens. Moreover, it was obvious that something peculiar was going on at Interior; the situation was clearly ripe for a congressional investigation.

To have an investigation, however, you have to have a committee. Unfortunately, Reuss did not have one, but he was a member of the Natural Resources and Power Subcommittee of the House Committee on Government Operations, chaired by Representative Robert E. Jones, Jr., of Alabama. Though Jones himself had never evinced any interest in Hunting Creek, he agreed to hold hearings on the matter at Reuss's and Moss's insistence. As things go in Congress, it was an act of courtesy and grace; Jones essentially lent Reuss the services and staff of the subcommittee. Hearings were set for June 1968; letters were sent out under Jones's signature to the Corps, requesting it to advise the permittee not to begin construction pending the hearings, and to the Governor of Virginia, informing him that hearings were to be held and inquiring about the status of the deed. Clearly such letters under the imprimatur of a powerful and respected Congressman like Jones were enough to insure that the deed would not issue, and that construction would not begin until the hearings had been completed.

Much of what the hearings revealed has already been indicated; in general, suffice it to note one Interior Department official's later observation that "the hearings were an emotional shocker for all of us." The principal victim, of course, was Assistant Secretary Cain, whose "flip-flopping" was the subject of much lively discussion and whose indiscreet memorandum, admitting that he had made "a decision based first on political considerations," was put triumphantly into the public record.

One matter that greatly interested subcommittee members was how Cain had happened to write the letter of October 1967 withdrawing Interior's objections. Had the Fish and Wildlife Service changed its position, they asked? No, it had not. Had Cain himself ordered or made a new field study, or had he himself reviewed the earlier studies, being an expert on these matters? He had not. Had he discussed his change of position with those officials before informing the Corps of this reversal? No, he had not. What, then, did inspire that October letter?

The first contact he had with the Hunting Creek matter, Cain explained, was "when this letter [withdrawing the objection] came to my desk asking would I be willing to sign it." The letter was written by Bernie Meyer, a lawyer in the office of the Solicitor of the Interior Department. Meyer had been asked by Bill Pozen, a staff man in Secretary Udall's office, to draft a letter withdrawing the objections. And how had Pozen come to ask Meyer to write a letter for Cain to sign? "I may as well explain," answered Cain, "I did get likewise from Mr. Pozen the sense that there was somebody that wanted this decision as fast as they could get it. . . . Mr. Pozen typically got numerous calls, handled numerous calls from all kinds of people on numerous matters. And he had been receiving calls on the Hunting Creek property." Who the callers were Cain did not know. "I'm glad I didn't ask," Cain said later, "I don't want to know." He told the subcommittee:

"As far as I know they could have been either pro or con the permit. This is a thing I did not inquire into." But he added: "I assumed it had something to do with the interest of the applicants." Pozen—who was never called to testify —later said that he might have talked to Senator Bayh about the case but did not remember. When asked to try to jog his memory about congressional phone calls on Hunting Creek, he replied: "I don't want to have my memory jogged."

Cain's remarkable lack of curiosity interested the subcommittee, but it was even more interested in learning how he went about deciding whether or not to sign this letter that had been presented to him with "a sense of urgency about the signing of it." Cain explained that he first went to see Secretary Udall, who simply said to him— without any sense of urgency—"This is in your program area, I would like for you to take care of it."

Then, as indicated earlier, without examining the technical studies which had been made by his own subordinates, without consulting them, and without making any investigation of his own, Cain signed the letter in what he himself described as "a decision based first on political considerations and second on the feeling that the values were not great in the area to be filled." Representative Vander Jagt asked Cain to identify the political considerations that affected his decision. Cain replied:

> There is only one which I can testify to. And that is the position taken by Congressman Dingell, in which he first historically opposed the permit, and then in a letter to the Corps of Engineers removed his objections. And I said . . . he is a great conservationist, and particu-

larly in the field of wildlife. So I depended very largely on John Dingell's action. . . . I also, as I said . . . had general information that the congressional interest was divided in this case.

Dingell's role in the controversy is puzzling. In May 1964 he wrote the Corps expressing "opposition to this proposed filling as being inconsistent with the public interest, dangerous to fish and wildlife, destructive of navigation on the Potomac River, and injurious to the interests of boatmen, water skiers, fishermen and other riparian owners up and down the river." In August of that year, after the proposed fill had been revised and reduced in size, Dingell acknowledged receipt of the revision and said he would review his position after he had considered the views of the National Park Service and the Fish and Wildlife Service on the revised plans. Later that month both these agencies reiterated their opposition to the proposed landfill even as revised.

Dingell was not heard from again until April 1967, at which time, though the objections of Interior to the landfill were still in effect, he withdrew his objections.

Dingell never responded to an invitation to talk about Hunting Creek, but in 1969 Cain gave his own speculation, noting that it was nothing more than that:

At the time Hunting Creek came up [Cain recalled] the Corps needed a place to dump dredged spoil near Detroit and Dingell had supported them in using a place that was harmful to the environment. Dingell probably wanted to be consistent—though he was a good conservationist, on this spoil matter industry was powerful. Dingell may not have felt he was in a position to object to Hunting Creek in light of what he had approved in Detroit at the same time.

The matter of congressional intervention was only slightly clarified by Under Secretary Black's testimony before the subcommittee. He had received phone calls while the Hunting Creek matter was in his office awaiting decision. He said:

> I received a telephone call from a Jerry Verkler who was a staff member of the Senate Interior Committee, expressing no concern on his own behalf but communicating to me that Senator Birch Bayh was interested in this, and he was more or less inquiring what the status of it was and who would be handling it. . . . [Then] Senator [Henry M.] Jackson, who is chairman of the Interior Committee, telephoned me in an entirely neutral fashion on behalf of Senator Bayh, emphasizing to me that he had no interest in the outcome of this whatever. He only wanted to be sure that it would receive a fair and impartial evaluation by me. . . . I had a telephone call from Senator Bayh himself, in which he expressed his interest in this development, in seeing that the permit was issued. He didn't—it was not in strong terms. He was hopeful that we would not continue to interpose objection to it, and I told him that it would receive fair evaluation. . . . The only Member of Congress who indicated he was in favor of it was Senator Birch Bayh. Congressman Dingell, while he didn't favor it, had quite explicitly withdrawn his objections. . . .

At this point Representative Paul N. McCloskey, Jr., of California queried Black:

MR. MC CLOSKEY: While the interest of Congressmen does not, and should not, affect your executive decision, I believe you testified you do keep a careful record of congressional inquiry and interest in matters of this kind; do you not?

MR. BLACK: Let me say, if I said that the wishes of Congress do not influence our decisions, I want to beat a hasty retreat, because obviously they do. . . . Ordinarily, a call from a Senator or Congressman does not slip my mind.

This little colloquy is a nice example of the public ballet that is so often performed before the decision-making curtain. It hardly lies in McCloskey's mouth to suggest that the interest of Congressmen does not and should not affect decisions, since it was being demonstrated that very day by McCloskey's colleagues that a scorned Congressman can be a very formidable adversary. At the same time, Black surely did not expect anyone to believe that telephone calls from the chairman of the Senate committee which principally deals with Interior Department affairs—calls simply to assure that an issue was being fairly considered—are routine events to which no particular significance is to be attached.

Black was being a little too clever. In admitting that he had received calls from Members of Congress interested in the grant of the permit, he made very clear that the opposition of other Congressmen, such as Reuss, Moss, and Saylor, had also been very forcefully brought to his attention. The implication is that both sides play the game, and such interposition is self-neutralizing. One may be permitted a little skepticism. It may often be that any decision will equally displease Members of Congress; it is not so clear that those who are equally displeased are equally important. And it is not likely that Under Secretary Black was insensitive to this consideration as he trampled around at Hunting Creek making that famous visual inspection. Surely he knew why Senator Bayh had thought it worthwhile to get the chairman of the Interior and Insular Affairs Committee to make a "neutral" inquiry on his behalf.

As one considers the implications of the testimony given by Black and Cain, it is less than comforting to recall how many and unpredictable elements there were in the events leading up to congressional involvement by those who opposed the project; in the opponents' willingness to continue their fight so diligently and so long; and—perhaps most significantly—how much more they had to do to get results than those who favored the project. It is striking that if Black and Cain were sensitive to congressional interest, as their testimony makes explicit, both resolved the matter in a fashion that pleased the Congressmen who were least agitated about the project, when it would have been so much more natural to oppose it, thus supporting their own staffs.

If their testimony is to be believed, the only congressional support for the project came from a few Congressmen who had done nothing more than write letters saying that they would not actively oppose the landfill; from Senator Jackson who said he had no interest other than fair consideration; and from Senator Bayh who made one phone call which Black had said—"was not in strong terms"—expressed hope that opposition to the project would not be continued. None of these Members of Congress ever supported the project publicly, commented on the merits, or deigned to indicate why or on whose behalf they had become interested. It is an interesting question, after all, why a Senator from Indiana should exert himself on behalf of a proposal put forth by investors from New York.

On the other side were a group of Congressmen with a continuing interest in conservation, whose opposition was perfectly open, and whose reasons for opposition were spread fully upon the record. A very curious business indeed for an agency that is concerned about "the wishes of Congress." More curious still was that no persons in the agency ever expressed the slightest interest in knowing why someone like Senator Bayh favored the project. Perhaps Bayh had some useful information or ideas which might have aided in making a rational decision. Or possibly he was simply conveying the desire of a constituent with an investment interest—in which case, of course, officials at Interior would have to give his view less weight than that of Congressmen whose opposition was based upon knowledge of the area and upon an opinion about the proper directions for federal policy as it affected the Potomac, a matter of continuing legislative concern. But as we have been seeing, this was a case characterized by nothing so much as a lack of curiosity on the part of Interior Department officials.

Inquiries to Senator Bayh were answered by his administrative assistant, Robert Keefe. According to Keefe, the Senator first became acquainted with the Hunting Creek controversy in the late spring of 1967. Bayh was in Indianapolis, and an acquaintance by the name of Mike Sperling asked him to look into the Hunting Creek matter as a courtesy to a friend of Sperling's. The friend of Sperling's was none other than John Schwartz of Columbus, Ohio— the man who later appeared at the Corps hearing to say he was one of Howard Hoffman's associates but whose interest in the project Hoffman denied.

Keefe said that he called the Department of the Interior in August or September 1967 to inquire about Hunting Creek and was told that except for some concern about the riparian rights of the National Park Service, the Department had not made any substantive judgment about the merits of the proposed landfill. In fact, Keefe said, he was led to understand that the Department had withheld making a response on the merits of the landfill for political reasons—that is, that it was reluctant to comment on the merits of the proposal because it was known that some Congressmen were opposed to it. He recalled being told that the Fish and Wildlife Service had taken no negative position on the project but that they had "a passive view."

Having learned this, Keefe said, he reported back to Sperling in Indianapolis that the best approach would be to get the Corps of Engineers to renew its request for a report from Interior and get that Department to take a position one way or the other. This was sometime in September 1967.

According to Keefe, the Corps then resubmitted the question to Interior and obtained the response that it had no objection to the landfill. The "no objection" response to which Keefe referred was presumably the famous Cain "reversal" letter of October 10, 1967.

The foregoing description may very well represent what Keefe was told, or what he recollected, of the events of 1967, but it bears little relation to the documented facts. For as of the summer of 1967 both the Fish and Wildlife Service and the National Park Service were on record as strongly opposing the landfill project on its merits. And both these agencies had reiterated their objections even after Hoffman reduced the size of the proposed project to accommodate concerns about riparian rights—which he had done almost three years earlier, in July 1964.

Obviously someone was very confused about something. In an attempt at clarification, Keefe was asked whether any efforts had been made on Senator Bayh's behalf to learn about the merits of the dispute. Keefe replied that he had indeed inquired into the merits and that it "looked as if Hoffman was getting a raw deal, and was being denied a permit for political reasons." The sources of his information, Keefe said, "were basically Ed Holland [a civil engineer employed by Hoffman as the project engineer] and other Hoffman people." Holland, it turns out, was an old friend and neighbor of Keefe's in Alexandria; and Stanley Bregman, the partner of Hoffman's Washington lawyer, Edward McCormack, was another Keefe friend of long standing.

Keefe had attended the Corps hearing on Hunting Creek in February 1968, but nothing which took place there would necessarily have alerted him to the strong opposition which the heads of the National Park Service and Bureau of Sport Fisheries and Wildlife had interposed to the project—for, it will be recalled, no Interior Department officials appeared to testify at the hearing; Assistant Secretary Cain had "decided there was no need to appear in this particular case." Subsequently, Senator Bayh, who obtained his knowledge of the controversy through Keefe, telephoned Under Secretary Black and, as Black testified, "expressed his [Bayh's] interest . . . in seeing that the permit was issued."

The background of Senator Bayh's interest in the Hunting Creek project was not made public during the legislative hearings in the summer of 1968, and by July the hearings ended temporarily. What had been revealed, however, was enough to produce "an emotional shocker" for officials at the Interior Department. Nevertheless, nothing that had occurred up to that time served to affect in the slightest degree Interior's policy position, that of the Corps, or—of course—that of the developers. Strictly speaking, things were just where they had been two months earlier. The developers had their permit, and while they were still under a request by the Corps not to begin construction "pending the subcommittee hearing and consideration thereof," they were legally free to begin. To be sure they still had no deed from the state, but since they claimed ownership of the area anyway, that lack was not necessarily critical.

The Hunting Creek controversy disappeared from sight until the first week of September 1968. The developers then notified the Corps that they were planning to begin work on the fill October 1, and a drilling rig was seen taking test borings of the shoreline soil. At this point Under Secretary Black made a statement which came as a great surprise to everyone who had read his earlier letter to the Corps and had heard his testimony. He wrote a Virginia Congressman who had inquired about the Department's position, stating: "Our clear preference that the project not proceed has been made amply clear to the Corps of Engineers."

If that was the message Black sought to get to the Corps, he had certainly been subtle about it. For his letter to them nowhere expressed a departmental preference against *this* project. It said: "This Department would, of course, prefer that there be no additional intrusions upon the existing Potomac environment. Our deferral in this instance is dictated solely by the circumstances. . . ."

With the developers announcing a plan to proceed in October—and with no indication that anyone was about to stop them—local opponents became active again, and the focus of controversy again shifted to Alexandria. For the first time, professionals came onto the scene—Ted Pankowski, of the Izaak Walton League of America and lawyer Bernard Cohen. They worked to organize diffuse local citizen groups. Three things were needed: a dramatic act to revive attention, a specific goal toward which all opponents could work concertedly, and—if possible—a means to avoid a *fait accompli* by the developers.

They decided to bring a lawsuit.[3] It was, in its own way, a brilliant tactic. The suit claimed in essence that it was illegal for the state to permit shoreland to be conveyed away to private developers and to be removed from the public trust. Like the earlier, though abortive, effort of Representative Reuss to introduce the issue of racial discrimination, the lawsuit brought another dimension to the controversy. The congressional hearings had pretty well wrung dry the dubious conduct of federal agencies, though they had articulated the implication that political influence was being applied to help some real estate investors make big profits. The lawsuit simply shifted this issue to the state level. Why had the Virginia legislature been willing to

[3] Fairfax County Federation of Citizens Association *et al.* v. Hunting Towers Operating Company *et al.*, Civil Action no. 4963A, U.S. Dist. Ct., Eastern District of Va. (filed October 1, 1968).

deed over such valuable land for such a small sum? And would the Governor really sign the deed after all that had now been brought out?

No one knows exactly what the filing of the lawsuit achieved. Those who initiated it firmly believe that it stopped the project from going forward, if for no other reason because it now put what lawyers call a "cloud on the title" of the developers to the submerged land, and that it served to prevent the obtaining of needed title insurance and financing without which the building could not progress. They also believe it gave the Governor—who had hardly showed any desire to take a leadership position in resolving the controversy—a basis for continuing to withhold the deed, pending the outcome of a lawsuit which would test the legality of his conveyance. It need hardly be added that the matter, as of the summer of 1968, was still under study by the Governor.

Lest it be thought that citizens concerned about conservation have the habit of running to court at the first opportunity without exploring more conventional means of redress, it is worth noting that in June 1968 Mike Frome (the outdoors writer who had caused Stanley Cain such discomfort) wrote a letter to a personal friend, Carlisle Humelsine, chairman of the board of the Virginia Department of Conservation and Economic Development, enclosing the article he had written on "the fiasco at Hunting Creek." He continued:

> I enclose also a clipping from the Washington *Post* of yesterday in which the developer announces that his next move will be to obtain a deed to the submerged land. I urge you to ask the Governor to withhold the deed

pending review, in light of the opposition of many citizens. . . . It might be helpful, Carl, if you were to contact Congressman Reuss regarding the law suit or investigation which he and his colleagues plan and ways in which the Board of Conservation and Economic Development can be of help.

Humelsine's letter of reply must be read at length to be appreciated:

DEAR MIKE:

Thank you for writing me about the Hunting Creek fiasco.

The events alluded to in your column . . . are indeed distressing, and I congratulate you on the eloquence and force with which you describe the problem.

My investigations reveal that the matter in question has been and is being handled for the Governor by the Office of the Attorney General. Under these circumstances, it would hardly seem appropriate for the Board of Conservation and Economic Development to intervene, particularly at such a late hour.

Of course, I have the right as a citizen to express my personal views to the Governor. Although I am deeply concerned about the problem you have outlined, I am afraid my personal appeal *now* would not be very effective. I believe it is wiser to hold my fire and save my ammunition for hunting game that might later prove to be more vulnerable.

I send you my best wishes.

Sincerely,
CARL

Frome replied on June 25: "The fact that the hour is late has not deterred a Congressional committee. It should not deter an agency of the State. . . . I earnestly hope that you will prevail upon the Governor. . . ." Frome wrote again in July and in October, both to Humelsine and to Marvin Sutherland, director of the department of which Humelsine was chairman. It all ended with a letter from Sutherland in February 1969: "Having read the transcript of the Hunting Creek hearings . . . I feel our Departmental position remains substantially the same as it was when I wrote you last summer. . . . Thanks for keeping us informed."

Only after experiencing the difficulties of other approaches can one begin to understand how lawsuits get initiated in conservation controversies. Exactly what the Hunting Creek lawsuit accomplished beyond drawing together the various citizen groups opposed to the permit will never, as noted above, be certain. At the same time it was filed—October 1, 1968—the Corps of Engineers again asked the developers not to proceed on the project until the congressional subcommittee had acted (the subcommittee report, expected to be issued in October, did not actually come out until March 24, 1969). On October 3 the developers said that no further action would be taken until the subcommittee report was issued.

With the revival and emerging coordination of citizen groups, local governments finally began to face the issue. In mid-September 1968 the Fairfax County Board of Supervisors sent the Governor a letter urging him not to sign over the deed of land to the developers. And on the twenty-eighth the Alexandria City Council, previously concerned only with sewage disposal, defeated by but a single vote a resolution that the Council request the Governor to withhold the deed.

If there was a fairly specific point in time when the balance of power finally shifted to the opponents, it was probably in that few weeks late in September or early October 1968. It took much effort by many people in a variety of forums, and—significantly—it took four full years. No doubt in theory there were many things that might have been done differently, or earlier, and perhaps would have been, had there been skilled and experienced professional leadership from the beginning. But there was not—there rarely is in controversies such as that at Hunting Creek.

The final outcome was now in the wind, but it was still to await some important events. When the subcommittee report appeared in March 1969, it was unyieldingly critical of the Department of the Interior, charging violation of legal obligations, bad conservation judgment, bad policy, and acquiescence in an unjustified giveaway. The report contained little that had not been revealed in the hearings, but its title left nothing to the imagination—"The Permit for Landfill in Hunting Creek: A Debacle in Conservation."[4] It concluded with the recommendation that the Secretary of the Army revoke the Corps of Engineers permit.

There was only one more surprise in store for Hunting Creek watchers. It was late March 1969. President Richard M. Nixon was now in office, and the villains of the Hunting Creek debacle had departed for quieter places—Stanley Cain was back at the University of Michigan as a professor of conservation, and David Black was vice president of the

4 House Report No. 91-113, Committee on Government Operations, House of Representatives, 91st Cong. 1st Sess. (1969).

Dreyfus Fund in New York. Dr. John Gottschalk of the Bureau of Sport Fisheries and Wildlife and George Hartzog of the National Park Service were still in office, and one day they were sharing a cab with Jim Watt, the new Deputy Assistant Secretary for Water and Power. Watt asked about Hunting Creek, and Hartzog said: "Let it go —we are all sick of it"—in short, forget about it.

A week later Gottschalk got a telephone call from the assistant to the new Under Secretary, Russell E. Train, inquiring about Hunting Creek. Gottschalk said: "It was messy and I'd just as soon not reopen it." And Train's assistant replied: "What can we lose if we were to reinstate Interior's opposition to the landfill?" New administration, new policy—Interior Secretary Walter J. Hickel could do worse than reverse, for proconservation reasons, a Udall regime decision.

Under Secretary Train himself called Gottschalk and asked him to draft a letter, for Secretary Hickel's signature, reinstating the Department's opposition. It was done, and, says Gottschalk, "I have never seen anything signed so quickly, with hardly a word changed." On April 3 Hickel sent the letter to the Secretary of the Army. It was a blockbuster:

> I have had an opportunity to review the facts. . . . As you know, on April 26, 1968, former Under Secretary Black withdrew Departmental objections. . . . The Department now considers the proposal as a needless act of destruction of the environment of the Nation's Capital, and urges reconsideration of the permit previously issued. . . .
>
> The filling and the subsequent construction of an

apartment building at . . . Hunting Creek is not in keeping with the widely publicized goal of this Department to preserve and protect the values of the Potomac River. . . . The Department intends to firmly contest any needless filling of the Potomac or affront to its landscape. . . .

. . . the Hoffman proposal opens the door to future enlargements. . . . The justification would be essentially the same, that natural values have already been downgraded by existing developments. . . . The door should not be opened further. . . . The unnecessary nibbling of areas of high public value must be stopped. . . .

. . . the area in question has not lost any of its value. It still provides a feeding and resting ground for migratory waterfowl . . . a vista across the Potomac . . . a natural margin for Jones Point. . . . The time has come for the government to take a firm stand to protect the fast-vanishing natural shorelines of our nation.

It all sounds familiar enough; indeed, it is hardly distinguishable from the 1963 report presented by Interior's staff biologist. Only the signature at the bottom had changed.

It was probably a good thing that Secretary Hickel no longer had David Black as his Under Secretary; for it was Black who told a congressional committee that "a return to the departmental position of blanket opposition to the permit would constitute arbitrary and capricious action." *"C'est la guerre,"* Stanley Cain had said, when contemplating the possibility that he might have to reverse himself. Another day, another firm national policy.

When the Corps of Engineers held hearings again on

September 18, 1969, public officials were virtually elbowing each other out of the way to express their opposition. Even the Alexandria City Council had voted unanimously in the summer of 1969 to inform the Corps that the City opposed the project. At the hearings state legislators, Fairfax County officials, Representative Reuss of course, a lot of local organizations, and—impressively for those who had watched the struggle developing—the new Assistant Secretary of the Interior for Fish and Wildlife, Leslie L. Glasgow, slowly and deliberately read Secretary Hickel's letter. It was quite a show. The applicant's attorney looked very unhappy, and it was some measure of his sense of the outcome that he had filed a lawsuit that morning challenging the legality of the Corps' revoking a permit once it had issued.[5]

In March 1970 the State of Virginia repealed the 1964 law authorizing disposition of the Hunting Creek lands, and on April 13, 1970, the U.S. Army Corps of Engineers revoked the landfill permit. Victory at last? Perhaps—but as the man said, "money can always wait."

[5] H. P. Hoffman Associates v. Stanley R. Resor *et al.*, Civil Action no. 2668-69, U.S. Dist. Ct. for the District of Columbia.

Chapter 2

The
Lesson of
Hunting Creek

I

Stories about corrupt administrators are rather easy to come by. Hunting Creek is significant precisely because it lacks this element. Indeed, if there is any sense in which the case is special, it is because the villains of the piece were persons of more than ordinary competence and integrity and because both their personal inclinations and the mission of their agency were in consonance with the values that they betrayed. It is one thing to criticize the Bureau of Public Roads or the Corps of Engineers for their tendency to encourage highways or dam-building or for their oversensitivity to those legislators who act as spokesmen for the interests that profit from such enterprises. It is quite another to find a situation such as that of Hunting Creek—a fiasco produced by an agency whose business is conservation and which was brought into landfill matters as a statutory consultant precisely because the Congress was worried about the Corps' unresponsiveness to fish and wildlife concerns.

Stanley Cain, after all, was no cheap bureaucrat longing for a job with the industries he had been hired to regulate

—he was and is a distinguished and highly respected expert in the conservation field, who later returned to the same university position from which he had come. Secretary Stewart Udall, who could not have been unaware of what was going on in the Hunting Creek dispute despite his official silence, was as conservation-minded a Secretary of the Interior as the country had produced in a generation. Under Secretary David Black is an honorable man. And Dr. John Gottschalk, Director of the Bureau of Sport Fisheries and Wildlife, whose peculiar mixture of personal and institutional loyalty conjoined with high-minded principle, is a fine civil servant. Ironically, it took the new Interior Secretary, Walter Hickel, who came into office over the loud protest of conservationists, to untangle the mess his much admired predecessors had created.

Hunting Creek is important not as a revelation of official venality, but as a classic case of "sub-optimizing"— that is, a case in which a decision was made that seemed best to those who had power to decide when all the many constraints, pressures, and influences at work were taken into account. From the inside perspective of a government agency, hard choices must be made. An agency has its own priorities and legislative program; it has conflicting constituencies among which it must mediate, and in whose eyes it must—for its own good—appear to have a balanced position; it has a budget to consider and thereby a need for friends in the legislature.

Such considerations need not be pondered as if they were theoretical abstractions. Let the players in the Hunting Creek drama speak for themselves. It is only necessary to go back to those eminently instructive subcommittee hearings of 1968. Representative Henry Reuss is questioning Dr. Gottschalk:

> MR. REUSS: If there were political considerations as the primary cause of the overruling of the Fish and Wildlife Service judgment, in your opinion, is that good government?
>
> DR. GOTTSCHALK: If we could put this on a hypothetical basis, I would be much more comfortable.
>
> MR. REUSS: I want you to be comfortable. Let us put it on a hypothetical basis.
>
> DR. GOTTSCHALK: I think there are undoubtedly situations which arise which require the Secretary to trade one kind of achievement, shall we say, for another.

Here is Stanley Cain, trying to explain what he had meant in that memo about "political considerations":

> I knew also—and this comes in the sphere of political impact—that there were citizen conservation groups which were very much interested in the preservation of this. And I have got a pretty good record of supporting and going with and belonging to these groups. But in this case I opposed them. . . . And in my personal judgment I did not think this was a very important case in terms of the values for wildlife that were related to these acres.

The irony is that from an insider's perspective, the Hunting Creek matter may have been rightly decided by Interior at each of its many stages. Taking account of the Department's diverse interests, it may have been tactically sound to withdraw opposition in October 1967, to reinstate it the following April when bad publicity for the Department was in the wind, and to stand together on the merits of its positions when hearings were held in July; and it may have been equally good strategy for the new administration—which did not have "a pretty good record of supporting" conservation groups—to reverse that policy in ringing phrases in 1969. This is the dilemma of the insider perspective.

Moreover, the bureaucratic perspective tends to intensify the problem of the so-called "nibbling phenomenon," the process in which large resource values are gradually eroded, case by case, as one development after another is allowed. The danger is that in each little dispute—when the pressure is on—the balance of judgment will move ever so slightly to resolve doubts in favor of those with a big economic stake in development and with powerful allies.

It is so easy for an administrator to adopt the position that this is the last intrusion to be permitted, that no bad precedent is being set, and that the line will be drawn at the next case. After all, taken singly, no decision such as that at Hunting Creek is likely to appear arbitrary; environmental problems, such as estuarine protection, arise preeminently in urbanizing areas where demand for development is high and where—almost by definition—the specific land at issue has long since lost its ecologic virginity. Yet the same influences which led to the decision that no objections should be interposed in that case are equally likely to apply when the next application—now in the comfortably vague future—is brought forward for decision. And will it not then also seem quite rational to approve that very small incursion, with the same reservations about its successor? There is no sharp, scientific line of demarcation; areas are only more or less pristine, and each case in a developing area is likely to be just slightly different than the one before it.

Thus, all the political and economic pressures which serve to tip the scale in favor of a specific project, though producing a seemingly rational result when considered in isolation, may serve cumulatively to produce exactly the opposite of the overall policy that the administrators want to achieve, that they are mandated to achieve by law and policy statements, and that they may think they are achieving. The greatest problems are often the outcome of the smallest-scale decisions precisely because the ultimate, aggregate impacts of those decisions are so difficult to see and the pressures so difficult to cope with from the perspective of the insider. It is much easier to tell a developer that he cannot dam up the Grand Canyon than to tell each real estate investor, one by one over time, that he cannot fill an acre or two of marshy "waste" land.

II

In these ways the administrative process tends to produce not the voice of the people, but the voice of the bureaucrat —the administrative perspective posing as the public interest. Simply put, the fact is that the citizen does not need a bureaucratic middleman to identify, prosecute, and vindicate his interest in environmental quality. He is perfectly capable of fighting his own battles—if only he is given the tools with which to do the job. And, as the following chapters will illustrate, battles are best fought out between those who have direct stakes in the outcome.

The case studies which comprise the balance of this

book are designed to show that the courtroom is an eminently suitable forum for the voicing of citizen concerns over the maintenance of environmental quality. The real virtues of environmental litigation have little to do with the common conception of niggling lawyers battling over the intricacies of some ambiguous words in an obscure statute. Rather, the availability of a judicial forum is a measure of the willingness of government to subject itself to challenge on the merits of decisions made by public officials; to accept the possibility that the ordinary citizen may have useful ideas to contribute to the effectuation of the public interest; and to submit to them if—in the rigorous process of fact gathering—those ideas are shown to have substantial merit. *Litigation is thus a means of access for the ordinary citizen to the process of governmental decision-making.* It is in many circumstances the only tool for genuine citizen participation in the operative process of government.

In this respect the case studies which follow should illuminate—and dispel—some of the canards which often obscure discussion of citizen participation. The citizen who comes to court in environmental cases has traditionally been told that he is in the wrong place—that he should take his complaints to the legislature. A careful examination of these cases will show, however, that the citizen often comes to court precisely in order to *preserve* his opportunity to put his case before the public. It is not the citizen plaintiff in such cases, but his opponent, who is likely to be undermining the opportunity for open and genuine public debate on uncertain or unresolved issues of public policy. Thus we shall see highway departments paving over valuable parklands because some statute gives them authority to "improve" the lands of the state; a federal agency prepared to sell public lands for timber-harvesting before the Congress has had a chance to examine the relative merits of logging as against demands for wilderness maintenance; and developers about to bulldoze priceless fossil beds at the very moment the legislature is debating their maintenance as a national monument. It is in settings such as these that one begins to understand the demand for judicially declared moratoria, or orders for legislative reconsideration, as part of the effort to assure that democracy is made to work in practice as well as in school-book theory.

III

The elaborate structure of administrative middlemen we have interposed between the citizen and his interest in environmental quality has had another pernicious effect. It has dulled our sensitivity to the claim that citizens, as members of the public, have rights. The citizen who comes to an administrative agency comes essentially as a supplicant, requesting that somehow the public interest be interpreted to protect the environmental values from which he benefits. The citizen who comes to court has quite a different status—he stands as a claimant of rights to which he is entitled.

The changed status of the proceeding draws attention to an essential element in environmental disputes. Environmental quality is threatened so often because we have not put any price on it or marketed it as we do ordinary objects of private property. Clean air and water, public beaches, and open space, for example, are treated as essentially free goods, and for that reason it is little wonder that they have been used extravagantly.

They are treated as free in large part because no one has been entitled to assert a right in the maintenance of those values; no member of the public has been permitted to claim a legal right to the maintenance of clean air or water in the sense that the owner of a specific tract of land may demand the protection of the values inherent in that tract. In short, we have neglected to develop a sense of public-rights consciousness parallel to our concepts of private-rights consciousness. As a result our public values are degraded with abandon.

This is no merely legalistic or technical distinction. It reflects fundamentally upon our ability to protect public resources (which is simply another way of talking about the environment), and it goes far to explain why environmental values have been so substantially impaired. To devise a theory of public rights and a means of enforcing them is thus an essential step toward protecting environmental values.

As the following chapters indicate, litigation promotes environmental values by putting a price on them. That price is not always reckoned in dollars, to be sure. A public shoreline or park, for example, may be insulated from developmental pressures unless and until the public—through direct legislative assent—is satisfied that this trade is worth making, just as a private owner must be satisfied with a trade for his property. Similarly, courts may hold that environmentally disruptive construction must be enjoined until conditions are fulfilled that will assure protection of the values threatened.

The price exacted for environmental modifications is

usually some form of genuine public assent, which may
be effectuated through the remedy of the judicially declared moratorium, or remand to legislative action, mentioned above. The enforcement of public rights, at the
behest of members of the public, is thus the application of
democratic theory to the allocation of natural resources.
The following chapters suggest how such techniques for
implementing the rights of the public can be worked out
in practice.

It should be clear from these observations that the problems of environmental quality management go far deeper
than conventional efforts to patch up the present administrative process. In an important sense, they require a
repudiation of our traditional reliance on professional
bureaucrats. For a society which is ready to recognize public rights can no more leave the destiny of those rights in
the hands of bureaucrats than it would leave the enforcement of an individual's property rights to some bureaucrat
to vindicate when, and if, he determines them to be consistent with the public interest.

Thus far neither our courts nor our legislatures have
significantly faced up to the implications of public rights.
They continue to be fixated on the administrative process
as *the* mechanism for identifying and enforcing the public
interest. The public remains an outsider, to be tolerated as
a recipient of notices and participant at formal hearings,
but not as central player. Elaborate schemes are devised
for studies by agencies and for coordination among them,
but the administrative agency continues to be viewed as
the key instrument of decision-making. Even the most
sympathetic courts today recoil at the prospect of questioning an agency's discretion or its supposed expertise

about the public interest. The public itself is thought to possess *no* expertise about the public interest.

The consequence of all this, as we shall see, is an incredible tangle of agencies with noble-sounding mandates and small budgets; court decisions which, in their reluctance to question administrative discretion, send cases back for interminable "further studies" or with directions for correcting various little procedural blunders they have made; and proceedings that go on for years—and even decades. And when it is all over, we have, as at the beginning, a decision reflecting the agency's response to *its* political necessities—its insider perspective about the public interest.

Our need is not for more or fancier procedures before the same old agencies—it is for a shift in the center of gravity of decision-making. The recognition of public rights can, to a striking degree, effect that shift. The following cases variously illustrate one important means for doing that job—using the courtroom as a tool to enhance the leverage of individual citizens and citizen groups.

Nothing in this book is meant to suggest the substitution of judicial action for legislative policy-making. Indeed, if there is a single theme in this book, it is that citizen litigation is designed to promote and protect the authority of legislatures to make public policy and to make it more responsive to the interests of their constituents than is presently the case.

Neither is anything here meant to advocate the abolition of administrative agencies. They have their place; it is only hoped that the techniques suggested here will help them also to know their place. They are the servants of the citizenry. Their planning and regulatory functions are needed elements of good government, but those tasks must never be insulated from scrutiny demanded by those for whose benefit they are performed.

Today the management of environmental controversies is in disarray. Administrative agencies have been gravely deficient, and public confidence in them is eroded to an extreme degree. Citizens have reached out to the legislatures for help. New statutes are abundant, but their rhetoric far exceeds their effect. Unable thus far to perceive the fundamental issues raised by the environmental mess, legislators continue to pile more and more burdensome procedures upon agencies whose problems are far deeper than procedural failings. New councils, task forces, and commissions proliferate, but they seem little more than a revival of old institutional mistakes with new names.

In desperation citizens have turned to the courts. Judges have begun to lower the technical barriers to citizen suits, but they do not know where to go from that point. They fear that they will be asked to become scientists and technicians—to have to decide the relative merits of various pesticides or how a pipeline should be built across arctic tundra. The consequence is delay, confusion, and general bewilderment.

This situation must not be permitted to endure. The chapters which follow provide a start in charting where we are, where we ought to go, and how to begin getting there.

Chapter 3

Why
We Are
Failing

Today it is everywhere conceded that we have mismanaged
the environment. Public dissatisfaction has forced officials
to seek out techniques for reform. The opportunity is
great, but unless the right questions are asked it may soon
be lost. We are losing it now because a fundamental mis-
conception dominates reform efforts. We hold stubbornly
to the faith that the administrative agency must continue
to be our central institution for environmental decision-
making; as a result we continue to assume that some sort
of patching up of procedures, of the way the agencies do
business, will bring significant change.

Reform thus consists essentially of three kinds of proposals. The first is a requirement, now embodied in many
statutes, that agencies undertake more careful and elaborate studies before they approve projects before them.
The second consists in enlargement of public participation, reflected by better notice of proposals, more public
hearings, and greater public access to official documents
and reports. And the third revolves around a variety of
reorganizational schemes, such as withdrawing combined
planning and actual construction from the jurisdiction of
a single agency, greater coordination among a variety of

agencies, each of which has an interest in a given proposal, and the creation of new organizations (such as environmental councils or commissions) that are expected to bring a detachment and objectivity so often lacking in traditional, old-line administrative bodies.

Each of these ideas has obvious merit in theory, and each has the potential for some improvement in the decision-making process. But, as we shall see, none of them gets to the heart of the matter—a fundamental realignment of power; and all of them continue to perceive the citizen as an outsider, the ultimate beneficiary but not an active initiator with authority to tip the balance of power.

The distinction between the theory of reform and its reality was nowhere better illustrated than in the protracted controversy over the proposed Hudson River Expressway in New York. All the formal tools for rational decision-making were there in abundance, yet they were as a shadow to the substance of what really mattered in that dispute. To understand the Hudson River Expressway controversy is to know a great deal about the misdirection of most contemporary efforts toward environmental reform.

In outline the dispute was simple enough. New York proposed to build an expressway from Tarrytown to Ossining along the east shore of the Hudson River, in substantial part by filling the river's shoreline as a base for the road. In essence, the objection was that the fill would adversely affect a richly productive habitat for marine life and that an inland route along other established highway corridors would have been preferable.

In many ways the expressway controversy was a typical highway location controversy of the kind which has provided the meat of so many environmental cases in recent years. It differed, however, in one important way—this was no quietly routine project, initiated under old statutes lacking environmental standards, where a highway department simply appeared one day with its bulldozers. Quite to the contrary, the Hudson River had been an object of extraordinary public attention and seemed to be about as well-protected legally as any natural resource can be.

Congress had specifically recognized that the Hudson "contains resources of immense economic, natural, scenic, historic and recreational value to all the citizens of the United States," and it required that all governmental agencies refer to the Secretary of the Interior any plan which might affect the resources of the Hudson before any final action was taken on the proposal. Other federal laws specifically directed the Secretary to take necessary action to protect threatened fish and wildlife, and the Fish and Wildlife Coordination Act directed consultation with the U.S. Fish and Wildlife Service and state agencies in order to protect against damage to such resources. In addition to the Fish and Wildlife Service, the U.S. Army Corps of Engineers, the U.S. Department of Transportation, and the Bureau of Outdoor Recreation all were brought into the expressway controversy, along with the usual panoply of state administrative agencies.

Moreover, the State of New York had created a special permanent agency, the Hudson River Valley Commission, with the express function of encouraging the "preservation, enhancement and development of the scenic, historic, recreational and natural resources of the Hudson River valley. . . ."

Beyond these formal strictures, there was an almost endless stream of meetings, public hearings, and legislative inquiries on the expressway proposal. Indeed, the public record would suggest that it was one of the most fully studied projects in the history of American resource development. The Assistant Secretary of the Interior for Fish, Wildlife, Parks, and Marine Resources, Leslie Glasgow, testified in 1969 that "within the Department of the Interior, the proposal has received thorough study." A departmental memo asserted that "no transportation controversy has been reviewed more extensively . . . than this particular proposal."

Yet local citizen groups were not satisfied. They continued to fight the expressway through both state and federal courts and finally got a judge to issue an injunction halting work on the road. A little background information may help to put this "thoroughly studied" dispute into perspective.

In June 1969 Representative John D. Dingell of Michigan, Chairman of the House Subcommittee on Fisheries and Wildlife Conservation, decided to hold hearings on the expressway.[1] The inquiry was understandable enough, for here was an area in which considerable legislative effort had been expended to produce acceptable and informed administrative decisions, in which there had been much public participation, and in which a number of presumably neutral or uncommitted agencies had been brought in. Yet the process had not mitigated citizen dissatisfaction. What had gone wrong? A great deal, and if the Congressmen had been listening closely they would have learned

[1] "Hudson River Expressway," Hearings before the Subcommittee on Fisheries and Wildlife Conservation, Committee on Merchant Marine and Fisheries, House of Representatives, 91st Cong., 1st Sess. (1969).

how wide of the mark they had been in their efforts to reform the management of Hudson River resources.

The hearings began, as usual, with questions designed to determine whether federal administrative officials had fulfilled the duties imposed upon them by law. Thus Dingell asked Assistant Secretary Glasgow: "Did your agency actually make an independent study and evaluation of the biological effects?" The question was an important one, for a central purpose of the Fish and Wildlife Coordination Act was to bring into play the independent expertise of both state and federal agencies—a goal which will appear particularly appropriate after the role of the state officials in the expressway controversy is revealed here.

Glasgow admitted that his agency did not make an independent study "as such." "They did a lot of consulting independent of anyone else," he said, "but to make an independent study, they did not." In response to persistent questioning, Glasgow admitted that the Interior Department had simply used data provided them by New York State and produced thereby a report which was "very nearly identical" to the state's.

Thus does reality make mockery of fancy coordination and multiple-study laws. Interior officials, however, were not content to suffer the investigating subcommittee's criticism in silence. The time, money, and staff required to do the job demanded by legislative standards is far greater than any legislature has ever been prepared to invest, even for the most important projects, and far greater than the political dynamics of such proposals is prepared to tolerate.

The fact of the matter is, one Interior Department witness said, that "duplication of effort between our biologist and the State of New York would be a luxury that we could ill afford." And Glasgow testified that "this Hudson River Expressway project was studied as thoroughly as the average and probably more so than the average fish and wildlife review that is made under this act." Just to study the direct fish and wildlife aspects of such proposals, he said, would require studies to begin "at the time initial plans are talked about: and then if you had a two or three year period you could come up with a fairly good study of conditions as they existed in the river and, if you were to require a complete study, that would take several years."

The prospect of accommodating resource-planning for such projects as highways in order to study requirements of this duration and of making available on a regular basis staff and appropriations to carry them out is hardly good. It is not that such very long-range planning and forethought is undesirable or that it is theoretically impossible —rather, it is simply unrealistic in the context of contemporary resource management, and those realities are not going to be legislated away by Act of Congress. In fact, the Interior Department was given only ninety days in which to comment on proposed filling in the expressway case, and though that time was extended briefly, it was clear that the Fish and Wildlife Service was not in a position to put a decision off for several years.

Moreover, a direct study of fish and wildlife effects of the expressway proposal was only one of a number of important matters which a thorough investigation would cover. For example, if Interior were to fulfill its duty to minimize harm to the River, one question which would have had to be studied was the availability of alternative inland routes where fish resources would not be harmed at all. Representative Dingell raised this point and found out that no study of alternative routes had been made by the Interior Department. "Do you mean to say," he asked, "that when you have the responsibility to comment on damage and destruction of fish and wildlife values and methods for the preservation of fish and wildlife values . . . you don't think you have to comment on alternatives?"

An embarrassed Interior official could only give a typically bureaucratic answer: "I think a reasonable man would say that you should. . . . I am just saying that there is nothing in the legislation that would indicate that." Not a very satisfactory answer, but staff people at Interior were in no position to undertake such a study, nor could it be expected that they would assert initiative to demand that the project be delayed until these questions had been asked. In the hearings, one official drolly expressed his "feeling . . . that the State Department of Transportation could have considered alternative routes more fully than they had done."

Lack of time and money and the disincentives within an agency setting to raise doubts and delay are themselves powerful indicators of the defects in the implementation of the goals and the legislation requiring coordination among agencies or elaborate studies and reports. In addition, when problems—any problems—are presented in a diffuse and unfocused way, as by asking someone to consider all the factors involved in any proposal, the problems are so open-ended as almost to defy resolution. One could consider issues on a matter like the expressway forever and never get everything done. Fish and wildlife, housing dislocation, demographic patterns, income redistribution effects, recreation, local versus interstate traffic, racial impacts, and dozens of other issues all could be studied for years.

There is probably not a development plan anywhere in the United States that could not be attacked—as objectors attacked the expressway plans—for failure to study thoroughly some issue. This is not to say that the expressway controversy was admirably handled by state and local officials—it is only to describe the reality behind the rhetoric of administrative reform.

The romanticism implicit in efforts to bring about thorough study and coordination as a routine matter in the administrative process is only one of the problems facing conventional reform efforts—and by no means the most deep-seated. Even if agencies had the funds and the staff with which to work, their perspective would inevitably intrude to raise serious doubts about the conclusions they drew from the facts elicited. The expressway controversy illuminates this problem, too, in most dramatic fashion.

During the hearings, Dingell and Assistant Secretary Glasgow at one point turned away from the problem of information that had *not* been accumulated and began to talk about the merits of the expressway proposal on the basis of information that *was* available. Dingell suggested that the loss of habitat to be incurred by the expressway filling, even though much information was lacking, was great enough to make the project highly dubious; Glasgow replied that the loss was not serious enough to get excited about. The delicious irony of this exchange can only be appreciated if it is remembered that both Dingell and Glasgow were significant figures in the Hunting Creek case —only there it was Glasgow who spoke for the Interior

Department, reinstating objections to the filling of 9.5 acres of quite degraded wetland with a powerful statement against permitting such precious resources to be nibbled away acre by acre, and Dingell was the Congressman who had withdrawn his objections to the landfill, which encouraged Glasgow's predecessor, Stanley Cain, to remove Interior's original objections. With that background, consider the following colloquy in the expressway hearings just months later:

DR. GLASGOW: It would be my opinion that after a review of this Hudson River Expressway and the elimination of most of the objections to that, Interior came to the conclusion that there was not really a great loss.

. . .

MR. DINGELL: . . . Isn't it also a fact, Mr. Secretary . . . that there still was going to be significant fish and wildlife damage?

DR. GLASGOW: I am not sure it is significant if you figure out the percentage of the area that is lost.

MR. DINGELL: Well, you are losing 350 acres of estuarine bottom.

DR. GLASGOW: That represents about 12 percent of that one side. If you project it to both sides, then you lose less than half that amount because the other side is a better side for fish and wildlife. But if you project that to the unit which is there, an ecological unit that is present in this area, then it drops down to a very, very small percent, less than one percent.

. . .

MR. KARTH (*a member of the committee*): Mr. Secretary, we talked about one percent . . . and I would agree with you that if that is really the sum total of the destruction of the ecological value of that area, it is relatively insignificant, I suppose. However, if you keep chopping away one percent each time, and I don't know who measures these things in such distinctive percentages, pretty soon you destroy a good deal.

All this must have sounded familiar to Glasgow, for it is just what he said in opposing the Hunting Creek landfill nine months earlier. To be sure, the expressway decision was not Glasgow's; it had been made under the previous administration, and he kept insisting "of course I wasn't there." Notably, he hedged on defending the decision made by his predecessors. He concluded his statement before the committee by saying:

> This matter has been given careful consideration by the Department, and the position taken by the Secretary is supported by the recommendations of the staff based upon their examination of the proposal. On the basis of these conclusions the Department does not intend to reopen its reconsideration of this matter. . . . We, therefore, have not attempted to reach a fresh decision on the merits of this case. What we have attempted to do is to verify that this matter was handled by the Department in accordance with sound administrative procedures. . . . With respect to the Hudson River Expressway, we are satisfied that this was the case.

Unfortunately, no one bothered to ask Glasgow why he had decided not to reconsider the merits of the case, as his Department had done at Hunting Creek. We do not know, but we can certainly engage in some informal guesswork. It will be recalled that the decision to reopen the Hunting

Creek matter was said to be initiated when an Interior Department official in the new Republican administration asked what there was to lose if a Udall administration decision were to be reversed on proconservation grounds. Apparently it was determined that there was nothing to lose and a good deal to gain. But the Hudson River Expressway case was rather a different matter, for the principal and determined advocate of the expressway was none other than the Republican Governor of New York, Nelson A. Rockefeller.

To appreciate fully the political milieu of the expressway dispute and its implications for the Interior Department, one must recall a little history. In 1956, some years before the riverside route for the expressway was proposed, it was urged that a throughway be built, as part of the federal interstate system, several miles to the east of the river—directly through the middle of the three-thousand-acre Rockefeller family estate at Pocantico Hills, passing within two hundred yards of Nelson Rockefeller's home and about one hundred yards from the house of Laurence Rockefeller. In 1958 Nelson Rockefeller was elected Governor of New York.

During the next few years, various proposals for relocating the proposed highway both east and west of the Rockefeller estate were made, among them a western alignment approximately along the route of the proposed river expressway. As late as 1962 the New York State Department of Public Works vigorously opposed the western route.

In 1965 Secretary of the Interior Udall wrote: "Frankly, I do not believe that a high speed Expressway, serving commercial and industrial traffic would contribute to this objective [of preserving the river's 'irreplaceable values'].

73

Indeed, it would destroy the very access that, wisely conserved and developed, could return the Hudson River to the people."

By the time the expressway proposal reached its final form, certain changes had been made, among them the conversion from a federal interstate highway to one financed wholly by New York State; additional provisions were made for providing riverfront parks (on land donated by the Rockefellers) and for increased access to the river. Those factors were often cited in support of the expressway, though objectors continued to ask—without getting any satisfactory response—why desired parks and access could not be provided without an expressway.

In any event, by 1965 the New York legislature had passed a statute authorizing the expressway. That law, the subject of much subsequent controversy, moved through the legislature at record speed. The bill was not calculated to capture attention. It lacked the usual descriptive title and route identification numbers which would have brought it to the notice of local legislators and citizens.

The bill was reported out of the state Senate Rules Committee on May 12, 1965, and on the same day received its second and third readings; it passed the Senate without hearing or debate. Fifteen days later it passed the state Assembly, also without hearings or debate, and the next day it was signed by Governor Rockefeller, having been sent down to him in New York City by special courier. A local Assemblyman who tried to recall the bill, noting that the road would run through his district, was told he was too late—it was already being rushed to the Governor for his signature. Two state Senators were later quoted as saying they had voted for the bill in error, believing it was just a routine highway study bill. According to A. Q. Mowbray, one of them said: "I have been deluded. I am ashamed."[2]

Later, Assemblyman Lawrence Cabot went to see the Governor with an armload of protest mail and submitted it as evidence that the expressway law should be repealed. "The governor just glanced at the mail," Cabot said, "and listened to my report. Then he said to me, 'That is odd. I haven't heard a single objection to the expressway.' He kept a straight face too. He added that he was determined to build the road."[3]

Of course, with the elaborate system of law governing the Hudson River, neither the New York legislature nor the Governor had the last word. Among the protective devices available was an advisory agency known as the Hudson River Valley Commission. It was authorized to put a temporary stop order on projects such as the expressway and to hold hearings. The Commission did do this but afterwards concluded that the expressway was not objectionable. The Chairman of the Commission, Alexander Aldrich, conveniently happened to be a cousin of Governor Rockefeller, by whom he—along with the other members of the Commission—was appointed.

Several months before the Commission held its hearings on the expressway, Chairman Aldrich wrote the following note to his cousin the Governor:

. . . Judging from past performance, my instinct is that the Commission will want to hold a public hearing on

2 A. Q. Mowbray: *Road to Ruin; A Critical View of the Federal Highway Program* (Philadelphia: Lippincott, 1969), p. 160.
3 William Rodgers, *Rockefeller Follies* (New York: Stein and Day, 1966), p. 179.

75

the Expressway. . . . I believe it is extremely unlikely that the Commission will disapprove the road in its final Findings. There is ample precedent for this kind of approval following a public hearing. . . . If all goes well, the chances are that the Commission will approve the road (possibly with some minor suggestions) on or about Friday, March eighth. . . . I have discussed this time schedule with Bert Hughes [of the State Transportation Department] and he agrees that it sounds reasonable. . . . [P]ublic hearings [by the Commission] . . . will not affect the construction schedule at all.

Indeed, Aldrich was not quite a detached person; but there was still the U.S. Department of Interior to rely upon. In January 1968 Secretary Udall had a meeting with several representatives of Governor Rockefeller. Though Udall had opposed the expressway idea in 1965 and had been quoted in 1967 as saying that his position had not changed, he had not yet received any of the Interior Department studies referred to earlier. A memorandum from the Director of the Interior's Bureau of Outdoor Recreation, in preparation for the meeting, recommended that Udall "take the position that this requires an on-the-ground look by some top officials in the Department and . . . neither favor nor oppose it at the present time. I think this would be tactically wise."

At this point, chronology becomes quite significant. On May 3, 1968, according to Harry Rice, Assistant Director of the Bureau of Outdoor Recreation,

. . . there was a meeting in Secretary Udall's office, and he had been briefed by Director Crafts . . . on a study that had been made of the Hudson River Expressway and at this meeting in the Secretary's office on May 3, and I happened to be present at the meeting, he asked the Secretary what his position was going to be on the Hudson River Expressway, and the Secretary hesitated for quite some time and then he said, "We will not oppose it."

The Interior Department prepared three separate reports on the expressway. One, by the Fish and Wildlife Service, has been referred to earlier as having been derivative from the work of New York State officials and was the subject of discussion between Assistant Secretary Glasgow and Congressman Dingell. Two others were prepared as "task force" reports by Interior's Bureau of Outdoor Recreation.

The Fish and Wildlife Service report was made for the Corps of Engineers as a comment on a landfill application pending before the Corps. The Corps' request for the report was made on April 22, 1968, and the Fish and Wildlife Service's comments were finally furnished to the Corps in December. The point is simply that the Fish and Wildlife Service study was still in process long after the Secretary announced to his staff that he was not going to oppose the project. Indeed, that announcement came on May 3, less than two weeks after the Fish and Wildlife Service had received the matter for consideration from the Corps.

Moreover, the New York State Conservation Department report on the expressway, upon which the Fish and Wildlife Service relied, was only presented by its author in rough draft form to his superiors on May 3, the very day Udall was saying he would not oppose the project. In all the extensive hearings and trial on the expressway, there was no evidence that even the New York report was brought to Udall's attention before he made his commitment.

It would be useful to digress for a moment at this point to comment on the New York fish and wildlife survey which, whatever its impact on Udall, was the source of Interior's ultimate report. The New York report was prepared by a biologist in the New York Department of Conservation who was given only one month to do his investigation and was himself unable to do a field study. He relied principally upon earlier reports, some of which dated back to the 1930's. So the information upon which the U.S. Fish and Wildlife Service relied was itself a hurried and derivative study. Moreover, the man who prepared the state report admitted that his mandate was not to inquire into the essential question which should have been asked, but only to determine how adverse effects could be minimized, on the assumption that the expressway would be built. Naturally, he did what he was told. He identified potential adverse effects and suggested "measures to minimize effects of the project . . . based on the information presently available."

While the state and federal fish and wildlife studies were under consideration, two Interior Department task forces were looking at the expressway proposal, principally from the perspective of recreation. The second task force was not even appointed until July 3, two months after Udall had decided not to oppose the project; it was headed by Harry Rice, one of the officials who had been present at the meeting of May 3 when Udall announced his position.

The status of the other task force was more ambiguous.

It had been appointed as early as February 1968, though its report was not filed until May 31. The objecting citizens tried—without success—to determine whether Udall's May 3 decision had been made prior to receiving *any* of the Interior Department studies of the expressway. In any event, Rice conceded that no Interior Department reports were discussed at the fateful May 3 meeting in Secretary Udall's office. What did happen at that meeting, he described as follows:

> The director indicated to the effect that time was running out on us, on the position on the application to dredge and fill. He more or less asked the Secretary what his position was going to be in point [of] time. The Secretary got up from his desk, walked over to the window and looked out and stood there for a moment, and then, finally, he said, "We will take a position of no opposition," and that was basically the entire discussion on the matter.

Whatever the exact facts as to whether Udall had any information from his staff before making his decision, it seems clear that he had other things on his mind in regard to the expressway beyond the studies that were—in any event—unfinished or nonexistent when he walked over to his window and made that fateful decision. It is a pretty good guess that what Udall had on his mind was Nelson Rockefeller, and that after the May 3 meeting Interior Department employees studying the expressway were unlikely to feel much incentive to consider arguments against building the expressway.

Perhaps Udall looked out of his window and saw the future—a telephone call which came to the Bureau of

Outdoor Recreation on August 20 from Laurence Rockefeller.[4] According to an Interior Department "memorandum for the record,"

> Mr. Rockefeller said that he was with his brother,
> Governor Nelson Rockefeller, and he was calling to
> find out the status of Interior's review under the Hudson
> River legislation. . . . They wanted to be sure that In-
> terior had not lost track of the application. He said that
> he understood the Corps was ready to move but could
> not do so until receiving Interior's comments. He added
> that he understood Congressman Ottinger was putting
> great pressure on Secretary Udall to oppose the Express-
> way and implied that Governor Rockefeller was pre-
> pared to exert counterpressure if necessary. I told Mr.
> Rockefeller that the . . . Expressway matter had not
> fallen between the cracks in Interior. . . . Mr. Rockefeller
> said he was glad to hear that the matter had not been
> sidetracked and would convey the foregoing information
> to his brother. I told Mr. Rockefeller that I would in-
> form the Secretary of his call.

[4] Mr. Laurence Rockefeller, in addition to being a director of the Hudson River Conservation Society and a trustee and founder of the Conservation Foundation, is also, according to *Who's Who in America*, "Chairman,
New York State Council of Parks; honorary chairman, citizens committee
on Outdoor Recreation Resources Review Commission Report; trustee,
American Committee for International Wildlife Protection; board of governors, Pinchot Institute of Conservation Studies; director, Resources for
the Future; chairman coordinator, White House Conference on Natural
Beauty; commissioner, vice-president, Palisades Interstate Park Commis-
sion; trustee, president, Jackson Hole Preserve, Inc.; trustee, president,
American Conservation Association, Inc.; trustee, vice-president, New York
Zoological Society; recipient, Conservation award, United States Depart-
ment of the Interior, 1956; Special Conservation award, 1962; Horace
Marden Albright Preservation medal, 1957; Gold Seal award, National
Council of Garden Clubs, 1963; Audubon medal, 1964."

The matter had not "fallen between the cracks." In July 1968 the Bureau of Outdoor Recreation prepared a memorandum entitled "Benefits to Rockefeller Estate from the Expressway." The memorandum concluded there would be substantial benefits—a fact that was probably not welcomed, for the Bureau's Director had asked for the memorandum to be prepared for "what assurances I [Mr. Rice again] could give [my superiors], if any, that Rockefeller wasn't receiving some benefit from the Expressway."

By November, Udall "made a commitment to Governor Rockefeller that he would not oppose the application . . . for the expressway." The Interior Department memorandum of November 14, 1968, an instruction for publicizing the Secretary's position of nonopposition, provides as neat a summary of the expressway dispute as one might wish:

Udall . . . does not want action on this matter too soon after the election and recommends about December 1 as an appropriate time for submission of the letter to the Corps.

The letter to the Corps is to give the rationale for Udall's non-opposition. It is to state something to the effect that while he initially had reservations about the expressway, he is influenced by the findings of the two groups that made on-site reviews of the Hudson and, accordingly, will not oppose. Udall's feelings are that his decision is a very limited one in view of the fact that the State and Governor Rockefeller have prime responsibility. . . . [A] press release should be prepared at the time the letter goes to the Corps of Engineers. The press release should indicate that the Secretary's decision is based on B[ureau] [of] O[utdoor] R[ecreation]'s recommendation or on the results of the two studies performed by Interior officials.

It turned out that Secretary Udall's instructions were not crucial—in 1969, the Corps was enjoined by court action from proceeding with the expressway. But that came as the result of an entirely different set of actions by an entirely different set of actors—as we shall see in Chapter 5.

II

It does not take much of a diagnostician to identify the disease which infected the Hudson River Expressway controversy. Its name: politics. Its carriers: Nelson Rockefeller and Stewart Udall. Its cure: *not* more studies, more commissions, or more public hearings.

Many people find the suggestions toward which this book is leading—an enlargement of adversary processes—most distasteful. Surely, they think, there must be some way to provide a more expeditious and less "polarizing" way to settle unresolved issues of environmental policy. The air reverberates with suggestions of independent councils of experts, ombudsmen, negotiators, and so on. Let them consider the expressway dispute. With whom would they have dissatisfied citizens negotiate, and what leverage for negotiation would they give them? How would they modify the public hearing procedure (there were at least five such hearings on the Expressway) to deflect the determination of New York officials that the highway be built along the river? How would they reconcile the popular notion that failure to obtain project information early enough is largely at fault in environmental planning with the fact that the expressway controversy was a matter of public knowledge for several years? Finally, those who cherish the notion of independent advisory councils must ask themselves by whom such pillars of integrity would be appointed, and how they are to be made immune to the influence which Governor Rockefeller was prepared to exert?

Certainly no one would assert absolutely that such devices cannot work. They can, and at times do. But it is most important not to develop romantic expectations, for most such efforts—because they are in essence elaborations or extensions of the existing administrative scheme—develop the same political symptoms which they were meant to cure. They only rearrange, or rename, the insider perspective which is at the root of the problem. They fail because they do not change the balance of *power*—precisely what the development of a scheme of enforceable legal rights, backed by judicial power, can do.

These observations need not be left as mere abstract speculations. We have a good deal of experience with government commissions, task forces, and councils. That experience, by no means wholly negative, should nonetheless suggest the limits of our expectations and the usefulness of another kind of leverage that can be applied when such approaches fail to live up to expectations.

We have already seen one such group at work, the Hudson River Valley Commission—and a pretty toothless dragon it was. Obviously not all such commissions will be headed by cousins of a Governor or a President, but the power of appointment is rarely wielded loosely by political leaders. To take but a single example, the Governor of Maryland in 1969 appointed a commission to "look into the whole problem" of the effects of nuclear power plants on water and air. The panel, composed mainly of businessmen, industrialists, academicians, and state officials, included no one associated with any private conservation organization. The omission would seem peculiar, but the chairman of the study group blandly explained that conservationists had been excluded because it was felt "they would prejudge this matter."

A high-level committee appointed to study the supersonic transport (SST) illustrated yet another facet of the problem. The study group produced a quite negative report, emphasizing cost and demand uncertainties, a balance of payment problem, environmental dangers, and only minor technological advantages. The chairman of the group, Under Secretary of Transportation James M. Beggs, prepared a "summation" of the report for the President. It "accentuated the positive, eliminated the negative," to paraphrase the old song. An alert Congressman noted the discrepancies and asked Beggs to explain. According to a *Wall Street Journal* report,[5] Beggs replied that the President had given the committee a very tight deadline, and a very rapid review had to be made by people, many of whom "had never addressed themselves to this issue." Their reports were thus "not in any sense representative of an expert view in these cases." Moreover, he is said to have argued, the committee's views were out of date almost before they were completed.

5 Alan L. Otten: "How Not to Study," *Wall Street Journal,* November 12, 1969, p. 22, col. 3.

All of which, as reporter Alan Otten noted, "suggests several questions":

> Did the President, before giving his go-ahead, read the entire record . . . or only the Beggs summation? How must the important men on this highly touted task force feel when they see their work counted as merely one of many "inputs" and the "least definitive" one at that? Most fascinating of all, how often does this minimal-impact fate befall other big buildup task forces—ones whose deliberations are not so engrossingly spread across the public record?

Occasionally the task force approach has a happier ending, but the successes themselves indicate how special the circumstances must be, and how rarely they can be relied upon, to overcome the usual pressures of special interests and bureaucratic traditions. The point is nicely illustrated by recent controversy over a proposed expressway through Baltimore. As reported by George Favre in *The Christian Science Monitor,* a planning impasse had been reached between those who wanted an expressway through the city and those who opposed it altogether. To resolve the dilemma it was proposed to bring in an outside urban design team representing a broad spectrum of disciplines, to let the team air all possible solutions publicly, and to put the final choice in the hands of a decision-making group which would operate in the full glare of public awareness.

As the concept was finally implemented, however, the team consisted of an architect and three engineers, who were authorized to engage other specialists but merely as consultants, not as equal members of an interdisciplinary consortium. Moreover, the design team was tightly limited in the scope of its inquiry; most importantly, according to Favre,

> the route of the expressway was preset. This in effect meant that the design team's function was to make a *fait accompli* as palatable as possible, but not to attempt to change its route . . . [and] no team member was to give out any information to the public. This last requirement was so patently opposed to the original idea of full public participation as to be almost a mockery.

Happily, the architect member of the team, Nathanial Owings, refused to be so bound. As Favre describes what then happened,[6]

> Owings . . . sent his men out into the neighborhoods. They attended innumerable public meetings, listening to what the people were saying to determine the "needs." At the same time they answered questions, in the process managing to impart a good deal of information about alternatives to the public.
>
> This procedure in fact violated the letter of the design team's contract, and Mr. Owings was called on the carpet for it by "the client," as the state is (often wryly) referred to in this context. At one point payments to Skidmore, Owings and Merrill amounting to $700,000 were held back.
>
> Mr. Owings, apparently unrepentant, addressed the Citizens Planning and Housing Association in Septem-

[6] George Favre, in *The Christian Science Monitor*, February 6, 1970, p. 3, col. 1; see also issue of February 9, 1970, p. 11, col. 1.

ber, 1968. Before an audience of 500, including the Mayor, he called the present expressway routes a failure and said they would be ruinous. He took the occasion to suggest a new southern leg to the expressway, avoiding the central city. He pointed out that it would save the middle-class black neighborhood of Rosemont and also avoid the aesthetically disastrous Inner Harbor crossing.

For this flagrant breach of the design-team contract the architect was threatened with dismissal. He capitulated at that point, but the yeasty process of public dissent was at work. In December, 1968, Mayor Thomas d'Alesandro announced that Route 3A, the one preferred by Mr. Owings, would be accepted and called this decision "final."

It was a clear-cut victory for "the architects" over "the road gang."

The victory was sealed in January, 1969, when Federal Highway Administrator Lowell K. Bridwell, as one of his farewell acts before leaving office, approved 90 percent federal financing of the expressway in its new route.

If we could confidently expect such consummations in every case, the nasty business of adversary proceedings would diminish almost to the vanishing point; but the Baltimore experience will not be easy to duplicate, and its critical element—an individual of extraordinary pertinacity and independence—can hardly be reduced to some regular institutional form. Plainly, if philosophers were kings, government would be a pleasant pastime.

The popular desire to see environmental problems re-

solved by prestigious persons of high status, without the
agonies of adversary processes, fails to take account of
another important factor. Even where individuals of
unimpeachable qualifications can be found, and where
they are able to rise above ordinary political pressures,
their resolution of controversial issues necessarily involves
the expenditure of personal or political capital which is
by no means inexhaustible. The achievement of Owings
in the Baltimore dispute would not be easy for him to
replicate regularly were he to be charged with the resolution of environmental controversies in Maryland day in
and day out, year in and year out. If he had that task, he
would be most likely to find himself in precisely the position of many public officials today—with many issues and
constituencies to balance and finding it necessary, as Dr.
Gottschalk said of Hunting Creek, to trade one achievement for another. In short, he would lose that most precious source of authority—his position as an outsider.

There is, in this regard, an unfortunate tendency to
equate the capacity of individuals or councils to cope with
the specific problems that are put before them with their
capacity to deal with the whole range of issues that need
attention. It is clear, for example, that the recent efforts
of federal cabinet-level officials and the Governor of
Florida to work out a resolution of the controversy over the
jetport near the Everglades National Park represented a
notable example of problem-solving relating to an important environmental issue. Their achievement made
headlines and editorial pages all across the nation.[7] The
difficulty is that the enormous energy and prestige invested

7 Washington *Post*, January 16, 1970, p. A-11, col. 1; *The New York
Times*, February 1, 1970, Sect. 10, p. 1, col. 1.

in that dispute will not, and cannot, be reproduced for each of the multitude of serious environmental problems that face us in each of the fifty states; nor is it at all clear that those officials will even be able to maintain adequate surveillance over the developmental pressures that will continue to arise periodically in the area of the jetport.

Moreover, those who are so troubled by the prospect of case-by-case resolution of environmental disputes, as such litigation portends, should note that resolution of the Everglades jetport problem does not solve generally even the modest number of airport location problems which are arising in dozens of places all over the United States. Some general lessons can be learned from the Florida situation, as they can be learned from any important piece of test litigation, but those lessons will not settle the specifics of where and how to locate another particular facility. And it should be recalled that a principal ingredient in settling the Florida jetport case was the investment of prestige and political power by very highly placed federal officials at least as much as it was the acquisition of scientific data; such elements of political influence are among the commodities in shortest supply, whose expenditure represents a very high cost to the society. For most problems we will not be able to call upon such resources; judicial time and attention may well be the institutional resources we can most prudently invest.

III

Another misapprehension which ordinarily finds its way into proposals for councils of wise men, or environmental advisors, arises from a failure to distinguish between the task of a long-range planning body, designed to suggest policy directions in the large sense, and a tribunal whose job it is to examine and resolve controversies over specific project proposals.

To the extent that such councils serve the former—albeit important—role, plainly they do not substitute for courts vis-à-vis the latter role. A body which is concerning itself with the formulation of a national fuels or transportation policy is engaged in an enterprise quite different from the resolution of immediate day-to-day controversies over, for example, an Alaskan pipeline, a jetport in South Florida, or the location of some highway in Colorado or Louisiana.

The two functions are certainly related in the large sense, but it is extremely important to understand that distinct tasks are involved. And this distinction says a great deal about the enthusiasm with which proposals for advisory councils are surrounded. The advantage of such bodies, it is thought, is that they avoid the delay, argumentation over witnesses, cross-examination, and evidentiary matters which inevitably infect the judicial process. To resolve particular disputes, however, it is not at all clear how such tiresome details of administration can be avoided. The problem is that the concept of a tribunal of wise men thinking large thoughts does not pertain to the very different problem of settling discrete questions—where shall *this* highway go, or shall *that* filling project be allowed.

Moreover, unless such councils are to become institutions of enormous size, it should be clear that even with the greatest wisdom and efficiency, they are hardly likely to be able to turn their attention to any but a small fraction of the great range and diversity of environmental issues. Here too somehow the notion prevails that a multitude of complex and widely disparate problems can be coped with by some single institution operating with a largeness of vision that can sweep away the painful necessity of large numbers of decisions having to be made one by one on their own merits.

The gap between the capacities of institutions we create and the problems to be solved is considerable. Nowhere was this better demonstrated than in the enactment of the National Environmental Policy Act,[8] which was signed by President Nixon on January 1, 1970. That law, widely hailed as a landmark achievement, had as one of its principal purposes the creation of a new Council on Environmental Quality, a three-man body appointed by the President to gather information, review and appraise federal programs and activities, develop and recommend national policies, and document and define changes in the environment.

Upon signing the law, the President said: "The environmental advisors will be assisted by a *compact* staff in keeping me thoroughly posted on current problems and advising me on how the federal government can act to solve them." To leave no doubt that the word "compact" was carefully chosen, Mr. Nixon added:

I know that the Congress has before it a proposal to establish yet another staff organization to deal with environmental problems in the Executive Office of the President. I believe this would be a mistake. No matter how pressing the problem, to overorganize, to overstaff or

[8] Public Law 91-190, 83 Stat. 853.

to compound the levels of review and advice seldom brings earlier or better results.[9]

Precisely what the President had in mind for the Council is a matter known only to him. The unwillingness to build a large staff has, however, more than merely administrative implications. To build an organization with a capability for independent analysis of the whole spectrum of federal resource activities would be an act with vast political implications. To give such an organization effective power to veto projects proposed by various federal departments— and that would be the effective role of an organization with a full working staff—would be to create an agency so strong as to be able to subvert the desires of such traditional power giants as the Department of Agriculture, the Corps of Engineers, and the Bureau of Public Roads.

Is any President ready to take a step of this kind? To put environmental veto-power into a single agency? Mr. Nixon certainly does not seem ready to move that far. And yet, without a staff capable of independent analysis, the Council essentially has to rely for its basic data upon the staff of the agencies and bureaus it is overseeing; without a staff large enough to take on regular reviews of individual projects on a large scale, the Council simply does not have the ability to supervise thoroughly.

What is more, the Council itself has taken the position that the advice it gives to the President is privileged and confidential. Thus the public will not learn about environmental positions taken by the Council but rejected by the White House. The Council's public position will in es-

[9] A few months later the Congress did create an Office of Environmental Quality, with some provision for a working staff (Public Law 91-224, 84 Stat. 91). Its fate remains to be seen.

sence be that of a spokesman for the administration, rather than—as had been widely hoped—a spokesman for the public, openly expressing views which might at times be at odds with the administration's position and thereby using its prestige and public constituency as leverage to induce the administration to adopt sounder environmental policies.

The Council's decision to work as a quiet voice of environmental reason within the White House has not thus far been notably successful. In testifying on the highly controversial SST, Council Chairman Russell Train conceded that there were many unresolved, and perhaps unresolvable, environmental problems. He testified that the plane should not go into commercial production until those problems could be resolved. Yet he entered no objection to an appropriation by Congress of some $300 million to subsidize prototype construction. One can hardly help but wonder why environmental problems should not be attacked *before* hundreds of millions of public dollars were invested in initial construction work, and one might have thought the Environmental Quality Council would be the appropriate agency to raise such a question. But, of course, the President has been a proponent of the SST, and a council that publicly put forward such embarrassing questions might lose its influence in the White House.

The other major environmental issue which arose in the first year of the Council's existence was the mammoth proposal to build a pipeline and road from Alaska's North Slope (where vast quantities of oil had been discovered) some 750 miles across the state to the port city of Valdez on the southern coast. Everyone agreed that the proposal presented an environmental problem of the first magnitude, for the oil would be transported at a very high temperature (about 170° F.) through the permanently frozen ground of northern Alaska. Large-scale construction in a habitat of this sort presents not only the danger of massive oil spills, but of grave environmental disruption: the arctic environment—rather like a deep freeze—has little capacity for regeneration or the ordinary processes of waste assimilation.

Environmental Quality Council Chairman Train first encountered the Alaska highway and pipeline proposals in his previous capacity as Under Secretary of the Interior and was instrumental in drawing up a set of construction stipulations to govern the proposed work. Conceding at that time that technological and environmental problems had not been "completely solved," he said: "To my knowledge, no private construction has ever been asked to accept such strong constraints or such continuing direct control by the Federal Government."

He may very well be correct, but the constraints to which he was referring—the construction stipulations—are not calculated to put environmental concerns at rest. By and large, the stipulations consist of "thou-shalt-nots" phrased in the most general terms, rather than detailed instructions which impose definite obligations. For example, it is stipulated that "in excavation operations, Permittee shall use construction methods that will provide maximum protection to animals and human beings" and that "Permittee shall consider aesthetic values in planning, construction and operation of the Pipeline and its associated facilities and roads."

There are, of course, many other provisions, some of which are more specific, but the excerpts cited here give a sense of their general tone. Suffice it to say that a tough-minded lawyer determined to protect his client's interest could think of a great many ways to tighten these "strong constraints."

While controversy over the Alaska pipeline and road continues to rage, the Environmental Quality Council has been quietly sitting on the sidelines—at least through mid-summer of 1970.

Though the Council has been less than a smashing success during its first year of operation, it is not the only "reform" produced by the much-praised Environmental Policy Act. In addition to creating the Council, that statute also imposed upon federal agencies generally a large responsibility for environmental study and reporting.[1]

To read the statute is to understand why it has been so lavishly praised. It seems to embody exactly the popular requirements for administrative reform and supervision with which this chapter began—that is, for detailed study and reporting in existing agencies and the creation of a new council of environmental advisors without commitments to any particular program.

---

[1] Among its principal provisions was one which directed all agencies of the federal government to do the following:

Include in every recommendation or report on proposals for legislation and other major Federal actions significantly affecting the quality of the human environment, a detailed statement by the responsible official on—

(i) the environmental impact of the proposed action,

(ii) any adverse environmental effects which cannot be avoided should the proposal be implemented,

(iii) alternatives to the proposed action,

(iv) the relationship between local short-term uses of man's environment and the maintenance and enhancement of long-term productivity, and,

(v) any irreversible and irretrievable commitments of resources which would be involved in the proposed action should it be implemented.

What effect has this landmark reform law had on the Alaska pipeline project? About April 1, 1970, it became known that the Department of the Interior was about to issue a permit allowing construction to go forward on a road, a principal purpose of which was to faciliate construction of the pipeline. Efforts were made by concerned citizens to get the Department to withhold the road permit until unresolved matters relating to the pipeline were settled.

Interior refused, though it was conceded that no one yet knew how, or whether, the pipeline would be constructed with adequate environmental protection. With the pipeline construction question unresolved, apprehensions were inevitably raised when it appeared that Interior was about to permit construction to go forward on the road. As a practical matter, to begin the building of the road, with the large investment it required in equipment and manpower, would inevitably intensify pressures for rapid action on the pipeline. It would also seem obvious that a government agency concerned about environmental impacts would make a concerted effort to treat the entire bundle of developmental activities as part of a single environmental question, rather than fragmenting them—as the Interior Department was doing—into separate, isolated questions of a road and of a pipeline. Unified treatment was particularly important in the Alaska situation, where federal authority over the pipeline could have been used to assure that an overzealous state government did not unwisely go forward with the highway on its own.

Citizen groups began to fear that federal control was being permitted to slip away; great quantities of material for both the road and the pipeline were being stockpiled in Alaska, visible to any person in Valdez or in the major staging area in Fairbanks. Many business people in Alaska had a good deal invested in the project on the assumption that it would begin soon, and there was no evidence that federal officials were discouraging that expectation—though internal memoranda made clear that many important issues remained unresolved.

In this setting, the question necessarily arose as to what impact the new Environmental Policy Act would have on the situation. As already noted, the Environmental Quality Council had barely involved itself in the hotly disputed question of imminent road construction. The Interior Department, however, with specific obligations under the new law, could not stand aside. Attention thus turned to Interior Secretary Hickel, the former Governor of Alaska.

To read Secretary Hickel's statements as reported in the press is to be convinced that he is fully mindful of his duties to protect the public interest, and he has said many things not likely to make him a darling of the oil companies. An examination of the Interior Department's actual work on the Alaska oil issue, however, is considerably less inspiring.

It will be recalled that the new act imposes upon federal agencies a most impressive set of obligations to provide a "detailed statement" on a broad range of potential environmental impacts from proposed activities (see page 95, above), among them alternatives, long- and short-range consequences, and irreversible commitments.

One of the first fruits of this statute was the Interior Department's report on the proposed Alaska highway. It has a great deal to tell those who put their trust in statutory requirements for administrative study and reporting. The statement on irretrievable commitments, an issue which is usually thought to be at the very center of rational environmental planning, is characteristic of the report in both style and substance. It is quoted here in its entirety:

> The commitment of resources that will be either irreversible or irretrievable are:
> (1) The *gravel* that will be used for roadbed insulation which will not be available for other purposes.
> (2) The road *right-of-way* itself that, necessarily, cannot be valued in the future as wilderness.
> Federal lands north of the PYK [Porcupine-Yukon-Kuskokwim] line are estimated to be 250,000 square miles, an area approximately half again the size of California without one mile of State or Federally owned secondary road.
> The use of 13 square miles, or 1/22,300 of this total area to establish the first all-weather secondary road connecting arctic Alaska with Yukon, and constructed under close Federal supervision and enforcement, is not an irresponsible balance between the economic and environmental determinants of resource allocation.

Using this approach, the Interior Department might be expected to analyze the loss of the *Mona Lisa* as a "disposition of a few ounces of oil paint and 620 square inches of canvas (used)." Museums, they might add, already contain thousands of oil paintings which cannot be simultaneously displayed and are regularly stored out of public sight.

Had not some private citizen organizations sued to enjoin issuance of the road and pipeline permit in the spring of 1970,[2] the road right-of-way permit would undoubtedly have issued within a short time. The lawsuit was an opportunity for the Department of the Interior, and even for the Environmental Quality Council, to put on the record their concerns—so eloquently expressed in the newspapers —about protection of the Alaskan environment. The answering brief filed by the United States in the U.S. District Court, on behalf of Secretary Hickel, was lengthy—much more so, incidentally, than the Secretary's detailed statement under the Environmental Policy Act. Its chief argument in opposition to a judicial injunction concluded with this observation:

> The financial disaster which would be suffered by the independent contractors . . . obviously would have a far greater harmful effect upon the economy of the entire State than would any interference which may possibly occur to the plaintiffs' aesthetic sensibilities. The Court is asked [by the plaintiffs] to prevent the economic development of the entire State of Alaska.

As conservationist Representative John Saylor said, "Why the rush? This oil has been in the ground for a billion years. It has been discovered in the last twenty-four months. Because a few companies have invested a lot of money is no reason . . . to lay down and play dead." Judge George L. Hart, Jr., of the United States District Court, no sentimentalist, granted the injunction. Just because someone has spent a billion dollars, he said, does not mean that he can violate the law. Judge Hart held that the requirements

2 Wilderness Society v. Hickel, Civil Action No. 928-70, U.S. Dist. Ct., Dist. of Columbia (filed March 26, 1970).

of the Environmental Policy Act had not been met, and it was obvious he had been persuaded that the development of Alaska involved a bit more than the "aesthetic sensibilities" of a few conservationists.

It may sadden the observer to have to conclude that administrators have to be bludgeoned into doing their job under threat of judicial penalties or that private citizens should have to undertake the burden of effective initiatives. But facts are inexorable; they do not become less real because we dislike them.

IV

Before turning to the question whether courts are equal to the task which administrative failure is thrusting upon them, there remains for comment the notion that increased public participation in the planning process at a fairly early stage—before positions have hardened—offers hope of avoiding the harshness which characterizes litigation or other adversary proceedings. The idea is attractive, but its practical implementation elusive. Is there to be some more-or-less formal proceedings at an earlier stage, or stages, in the planning process to which the general public is to be made a party? And if so, is something to be decided at such proceedings, or are they simply to be explanatory, informational public meetings?

Expressions of support for a right of participation do not make clear the answers to these questions. If it is thought that decisions—of a sort which would substitute ultimately for the need to resort to litigation—are to be made at some earlier stage in planning, the proponents of any such schemes will have to confront the troublesome dilemma to which lawyers give the name "ripeness." That is, the more one moves back from specific and clear-cut proposals toward the formative stages, the more difficult it is to get anything decided because of the large elements of uncertainty and speculation. Thus, say lawyers, a proposal which lacks definition and specificity is not "ripe" for settlement.

For example, a public proceeding called to consider the broad question whether some new highway ought to be built in the area of the proposed Hudson River Expressway is likely to be pretty formless. It might help men of good will understand something about community feelings, but it is unlikely to settle anything about which there are firm differences or even to make very clear what those differences are. One can expect such proceedings to be diffuse, exploratory meetings in which there is some exchange of information about basic plans and some opportunity for various groups to begin organizing themselves for further study and action. Such proceedings will essentially elucidate problems, rather than resolve them.

The scope of the problem was indicated when the Federal Highway Administration, after much debate, issued a memorandum in January 1969 calling for two-stage public hearings on proposed highways. Previously only a single hearing had been required after a specific route had been designated. Under the new procedure there is to be a hearing on general location issues prior to the selection of a route and later another hearing on the design details of the road.

The original two-stage hearing proposal was vigorously opposed by state highway officials and the road-building industry; but they finally agreed to an amended version which omitted a right of "any interested person" to appeal location and design decisions. A spokesman for the American Road Builders Association was quoted as saying that the final version "answered our principal objections." Conversely, Spencer Smith of the Citizens' Committee on Natural Resources called the amendment "a complete and total victory for the highway lobby." Plainly those who participate in such controversies recognize that the opportunity, ultimately, to obtain some form of external review is the critical issue. Proposals for friendly mediation, however elaborately devised, will not prevent serious conflicts or the need for a forum to resolve them.

The idea of a right to participate in planning has another difficulty as well. The planning process is obviously a continuous one, often extending over a number of years and rarely having clearly definable points at which critical decisions are made. It is unlikely that a process so amorphous can be reduced to any satisfactory set of rules which would truly bring a broader range of citizen perspective into the actual process of decision-making. So much in the real planning process is done by informal conversation and consultation, and there is a kind of wishfulness in feeling that by legal rules or institutional manipulation the "insider perspective" can be reformed and legislated into that all-embracing public interest perspective which is our ideal.

Indeed, a basic difficulty is that the agencies' self-interest encourages them to confront the public with a *fait accompli*. Both public and private agencies are well aware of the benefits of surprise and of the weight that tends to be given the argument that much time, effort, and money has *already* been invested in a proposal. Thus, to protect themselves from attacks on their plans, agencies traditionally have been very reluctant to share their planning process with elements of the public which might become adversaries.

Such agency self-protectiveness does pay practical dividends for entrepreneurs. In the planning for offshore oil drilling at Santa Barbara, for example, the oil companies made much of the fact that *by the time* citizens began to complain, they had already invested millions of dollars in exploratory work and that it was by then too late to begin reexamining the proposal to drill. Plainly it was in their interest to keep public concern from arising until they were in a position to make this argument. Similarly, in a widely publicized dispute involving a chemical company's desire to build a plant on the South Carolina coast, citizens who finally heard of the proposal and began to organize opposition, discovered that the chemical company had earlier quietly obtained the acquiescence of South Carolina officials. Their approval was a powerful lever in favor of the company, which only a massive publicity and legal campaign by local opponents of the plant subsequently undermined.[3] Had public opposition arisen earlier, officials would most likely have felt compelled to take at least a neutral stand.

These same surprise tactics are often used by public agencies, which suddenly appear with a bulldozer, play down rumors of impending land condemnations, or argue —when challenged—that huge sums have already been invested and that public opposition (which they have muted by their own tactics) comes too late. An eminent

[3] See, for example, *Life Magazine,* January 30, 1970, pp. 22-30; the litigation involved is Hilton Head Fishing Cooperative *et al* v. BASF Corporation, Civil Action No. 70-105, U.S. Dist. Ct., S.C. (Amended Complaint filed March 3, 1970).

practitioner of such stratagems was Robert Moses, New York's Commissioner of Just About Everything. One well-known case in point occurred some years ago, when Moses's plan to build a parking lot in Central Park was temporarily stymied by irate mothers who came out in force—with baby carriages—to stand in front of the bulldozers. The ladies had their way for a while. A few days later, at one a.m., while picketers and children slept, Commissioner Moses moved in the bulldozers; when the mothers arrived to resume their vigil the next morning, a fence was up and a number of trees were down. Dramatic newspaper coverage and an imaginative appeal to the courts saved the parkland at the last moment, no thanks to Moses, who described his opponents as "a small, noisy minority . . . of childless women howling about their non-existent children."[4]

Despite all these difficulties, the agencies should continue to be encouraged to promote greater citizen participation during the formative stages of their planning, for such participation will at least alert citizens to the problems they face and to the need for further action. Public participation in the administrative process is necessary, but it is *not* sufficient. The following measures should, therefore, be taken:

Agencies should be required to make their planning studies and other such documents more widely available —the federal Freedom of Information Act is a helpful step in this direction—current notions and practices about confidentiality and privilege are too rigorous. The availability of such information will promote opportunities for citizen

4 John B. Keeley: *Moses on the Green,* Inter-university Case Program Studies (Indianapolis: Bobbs-Merrill, 1959).

groups to engage in their own parallel and simultaneous analyses, leading to alternative solutions which can be put before the public and legislatures as a foil to officially produced plans.

Where officially sanctioned outside groups can be formed to study alternatives—as occurred in the Baltimore highway dispute—that approach should be taken. The presence of such alternative plans may itself carry enough weight to stop unwise proposals by public and private entrepreneurs. Such a study was used successfully to raise serious doubts about a proposed nuclear plant on Lake Cayuga in New York State.[5] Several alternatives were produced in the Everglades jetport controversy mentioned earlier—both public and private study groups conducted surveys and put their proposals before the public. Most surveys, task force reports, and the like, however, are still studiously ignored and left to the oblivion of some library shelf. Ultimately, therefore, an opportunity must be left for the presentation of such alternative plans in a courtroom setting.

Public hearings are also desirable, as indicated above, so long as it is understood that they serve principally as forums to marshal and elucidate the available facts and to provide a focus for citizen organization, rather than as substitutes for conflict resolution of the sort carried out by courts. It seems undesirable, however, to burden every public agency with fixed requirements that they hold hearings routinely on each of the enormous number of their decisions which have potential environmental effects. The approach of the Corps of Engineers in certain of its func-

[5] *Wall Street Journal*, April 14, 1970, p. 7, col. 1.

tions—to hold a hearing when there is substantial local objection—is more sensible. Agencies should not be saddled with unrealistic and unnecessarily elaborate procedures, which usually turn out to have more form than substance.

To any official agency approach, an opportunity for citizen-initiated hearings, upon petition by a substantial number of persons, should be added. Of course, as we have seen, any such scheme presents difficulties. Lest such demands on agencies proliferate unreasonably, it is necessary to identify certain points in the planning process when a hearing could be held—such as on the completion of a planning report or survey, the decision to open an area for bidding, or the determination to let a contract. The requirement of a hearing contingent upon substantial petition would be some deterrent to abuse, and so long as the challenged agency itself ran the hearings, there would be some constraint on unreasonable citizen demands. As with other elements of the environmental problem, the goal is to produce new leverage for private initiatives, and toward that goal some of the risks of building an open-ended system are worth taking.

Yet another idea, often advanced, is that litigation could be averted if a new institution were created to provide a form of administrative adjudication, with personnel drawn from outside the challenged agency. This would, it is true, mitigate the conflict of interest which one now finds in agency-run public hearings. Experience suggests, however, that such an approach does not ultimately make litigation unnecessary—it only adds another level of administration and delay. It is virtually a truism among those who deal with the administrative process that the decisions of such boards of review are inevitably taken to litigation anyway when matters of importance are at stake. This is very generally the case with existing boards of review in agencies like the Interior Department, as it is with more elaborate agencies such as the Federal Power Commission.

It is most unclear what gain is thought to be had by proliferating such boards. If they engage in careful review, with adequate protection for all parties, they tend to have all the disadvantages of a court—delay and complex procedures. Moreover, contemporary environmental disputes are not of a kind where technical competence is central; they are essentially controversies over policy choices. And, most importantly, such boards of review have all the problems of personnel selection which infect present administrative agencies, with the advantage of only limited insider perspective: they may become the captives of the industries they regulate—their very specialization means that they are likely to bring a particular perspective to bear on environmental problems and to be selected for the job with that in mind. Conversely, environmental problems will never be a principal part of the courts' business, and for problems in which political pressures are a central issue, this diversity of matters before a court is an advantage of the greatest possible significance.

To be sure, courtroom proceedings are harsh and unforgiving, unlike the friendly mediation sessions and elegant study projects of which so many social planners' dreams are made. But environmental problems breed determined adversaries; the need is for institutions that know how to expose and resolve, unsentimentally, the elemental issues in a dispute. For this task the courts are uniquely qualified.

Chapter 4

A Role
for the
Courts

I

What have courts to offer in the resolution of environmental disputes that other institutions, such as those discussed in the preceding chapter, lack? Certainly judges are no wiser in such matters than those who hold administrative posts. They are no less amenable to corruption. Nor, certainly, are they better equipped to design highways or pipelines.

The judiciary has several virtues which have thus far been largely lacking in those who attempt to deal with environmental quality. First, judges are outsiders. The amenability to political pressures of the kind which loomed so large in controversies like Hunting Creek and the Hudson River Expressway, and which were critical in those cases, except in the rarest situations has no place in the judicial process. Judges do not ordinarily receive telephone calls from Senators or the brothers of Governors, and they do not have an agency's program or budget to balance against the merits of a particular case. All the things which make an administrative agency so much a political institution, as indicated in the preceding chapters, are essentially lacking in the courts. In this respect, a change of institutions can be more than a change of form—it gets to the heart of the matter, the problem of insider perspective.

The court is an outsider in another sense as well, which distinguishes it from even new organizations like the Environmental Quality Council. Judges, as stated in Chapter 3, will spend only a tiny fraction of their time and energy dealing with environmental disputes. For this reason the process of judicial selection is not significantly affected by anyone's estimate of a given judge's attitudes about those issues. This is a most important fact, one which can hardly be applied to any institution that deals regularly with environmental matters. A President or a Governor who is choosing an environmental council cannot avoid consideration of the attitude that important interest groups—whether the oil industry or conservation organizations—will adopt toward that choice. But the very diversity of the judicial role and the large numbers of judges among whom such cases will be divided tend to reduce this consideration virtually to the zero point. And this, of course, is a tremendously liberating factor when one considers the political dimension that plays so important a role in the administrative process. While judicial selection is itself tempered by consideration of matters which dominate the attention of courts, such as the criminal law, a judge's attitudes about law and order (for example) in no way necessarily affect his judgments about potential environmental cases. This is a valuable advantage, and it should be exploited.

By the same token, the breadth of judicial work and diffusion of environmental issues among many courts and judges, free any given judge very substantially from the concerns which inevitably affect a specialized administrator or advisor, particularly the need to maintain some sort of politically balanced position among the constituencies with which he regularly deals. Assistant Secretary of the Interior Stanley Cain's revealing comment in the context of Hunting Creek as to his general reputation among conservationists (see page 54, above) makes the point clear. Any official who deals routinely with particular interest groups inevitably feels the need to do some "trading" in order to maintain a credible position in the eyes of those constituencies. This pressure towards sub-optimizing too is virtually absent in the judicial process.

It may seem a paradox that the greatest strength of an institution is its lack of expertise, that quality much vaunted among administrators, but to understand and appreciate this paradox is to understand the heart of the administrative dilemma—the problem of the insider viewpoint. The issue of expertise, and whether judges are to be asked to design bridges and power plants, will be dealt with at length in the chapters which follow; for the moment, suffice it to note that those who actually make the decisions in controversial environmental cases turn out ordinarily not to be technical experts, making technical decisions, but (most frequently) lawyers in high positions making policy judgments. Recall the comments of lawyer-Under Secretary Black in the Hunting Creek case (page 27, above) and lawyer-Secretary Udall looking out the window and deciding the Hudson River Expressway question (page 79, above).

Yet another virtue of the judicial process, and perhaps the most important, is the opportunity which the lawsuit provides for private-citizen initiatives. In the preceding chapter it was noted that one must distinguish between the ability of agencies or officials to cope with problems they have undertaken to resolve (such as the Everglades jetport dispute) and their inability to cope with *all* the issues which deserve attention. Plainly, one of the greatest difficulties is in getting a dispute upon the action agenda of an environmental council, a highly placed official, or a congressional committee. Not only are time and energy limited, but the very pressures which lead in the first instance to questionable decisions often serve to make it imprudent for agencies or officials to take needed initiatives.

It is in this respect that courts are perhaps outstandingly unique. In a lawsuit no public official need take any initiative. A case is instituted by private citizens who feel they have a legitimate grievance. The court is spared the responsibility for opening sensitive questions—indeed, in a number of environmental lawsuits, judges have made it a point to comment from the bench that they do not seek out controversies and would be just as happy to be left alone, but that if a citizen comes to them with a complaint, they have a duty to respond. Moreover, the traditional legal process is particularly responsive to this problem of citizen initiative. Not only is there no "political screening" of cases, but once a complaint is filed, the judicial process moves inexorably forward. Pleadings are filed, testimony taken, requests for particular relief are put forward and must be acted upon. It is not in the nature of the judicial process—as it so often is with complaints made elsewhere in the governmental system—for a matter to be shelved, put off for interminable study, or met with a form letter noting that some official is glad to hear of the matter and will certainly give it his consideration (someday, maybe).

These elements of the judicial process strongly support the need, adverted to earlier, for citizens to feel that they are not merely passive bystanders in making their government work. The opportunity for anyone to obtain at least a hearing and honest consideration of matters that he feels important must not be underestimated. The availability of a judicial forum means that access to government is a reality for the ordinary citizen—that he can be heard and that, in a setting of equality, he can *require* bureaucrats and even the biggest industries to respond to his questions and to justify themselves before a disinterested auditor who has the responsibility and the professional tradition of having to decide controversies upon the merits. The citizen asserts rights which are entitled to enforcement; he is not a mere supplicant.

As we shall see later, the judicial process also demands that controversies be reduced to rather concrete and specific issues rather than allowed to float around in the generality that so often accompanies public dispute. It is easy for agencies to put off decisions by throwing into the controversy some vague comments about "loss of jobs," or "world oil supplies," or "building a tax base." Judges, on the other hand, must make specific decisions, and those who appear before them are necessarily required to shape their controversies to precise, manageable issues that can be the subject of specific orders. This is not to say that large issues, such as population control, ought to have no forum. Quite the contrary, it is to suggest the usefulness of a forum which permits us to *begin* examining those large and underlying issues in discrete and manageable contexts. It is to move toward the general through the specific. We have far too little of this sort of public debate, and the opportunity to enhance such particularized resolution of disputes is nowhere better presented than by the courts.

Finally, it should again be made clear that to enlarge the ambit of judicial activity in environmental matters is not to restrict or supplant other modes for public debate or the resolution of controversy. Administrative regulation will go on, legislative standards will be set, hearings and investigations will continue. Task forces and advisory panels will continue to engage in both long-range planning and some degree of specific dispute management. Courts serve only to supplement these activities and to encourage them to be carried forward more adequately in the knowledge that there remains another source of redress and review when they can be shown to be inadequate.

In this regard, it is essential to understand that litigation is not antithetical to planning. Indeed, one of its principal functions is to promote intelligent planning and the consideration of large, long-range issues. The principal function of courts in environmental matters is to restrain projects that have not been adequately planned and to insist that they not go forward unless and until those who wish to promote them can demonstrate that they have considered, and adequately resolved, reasonable doubts about their consequences. Similarly, courts frequently require fuller and more open public debate (as by a remand to the legislature) in cases in which action is about to be undertaken before important policy matters have been satisfactorily resolved. In this sense, courts exercise an overview designed to assure that democratic processes are made to work and reflect the full range of public attitudes.

In the largest and most important sense, judicial intervention forces officials to take into account the wide implications and consequences of their proposals by challenging them at the operative level. For example, no one would expect a court to enjoin the federal highway program in general and order that the funds be reallocated to a more effective program of mass transit. But by restraining particular elements of that program, where inadequate provision has been made for accommodating public dissatisfactions or for taking into account the potential losses to important public resources such as parks and open space, congestion, noise, and air pollution, the courts thrust back on the highway builders some of the difficulties that the "true cost" of their proposal imply. To the extent that this sort of judicial activity requires officials to consider alternatives, such as mass transportation schemes, which may then seem relatively less costly, the courts have helped to promote precisely the sort of broad planning that we all approve but find it so difficult to implement through traditional institutions.

The same sort of analysis may be made of private enterprises. Companies engaged in the production of electric power lament the constraints that judicial intervention has imposed upon their planning. On the other side, many wonder how we can ever bring home to the public the true costs of ever-increasing demands for electric power. The courts help to focus the issue. By imposing restraints on the construction of new facilities that inadequately compensate for losses in public amenities and natural habitats, they discourage to an extent the traditional search for ever more power. In so doing, they encourage the search for less costly—that is, less harmful—solutions, and they have the power to transform the sense of urgency about the need for such solutions from rhetoric to reality.

Litigation, then, provides an additional source of leverage in making environmental decision-making operate rationally, thoughtfully, and with a sense of responsiveness to the entire range of citizen concerns. Courts alone cannot and will not do the job that is needed. But courts can help to open the doors to a far more limber governmental process. The more leverage citizens have, the more responsive and responsible their officials and fellow citizens will be.

II

The merits of judicial action must necessarily be tested against customary fears that the lawsuit engenders interminable delay, acts as an invitation to cranks, and is, at best, a two-edged sword by which those who wish to impede rational planning will be empowered to the same degree as those who desire to advance it.

The problem of delay is widely misunderstood and must be clarified in light of the kind of judicial intervention that is of principal concern here. Courts generally are able to grant two basic types of relief: remedies for past or continuing harm, in the form of money damages or an order to take remedial action (such as construction of pollution control facilities) ; and preventive relief, in the form of an injunction against proposed activity.

This book deals principally with preventive injunctions,

designed to stop environmentally dangerous projects before
they get underway. And, within that category, it attends
primarily to cases in which immediate judicial restraints
are sought against conduct that is about to go forward quite
soon. The implications of this for the usual problems of
delay are obvious. Such immediate injunctive relief by its
very nature must be made available quickly and is usually
obtained within a matter of days, or weeks at the most. The
primary function of plaintiffs in such a setting is to establish
that they have a significant interest at stake that is likely
to be seriously threatened unless the proposed activity is
withheld until the full merits of the controversy can be
fully considered. Thus, from the point of view of potential
plaintiffs advocating environmental protection, delay in
getting heard is not a serious problem. Indeed, the opportunity for speedy relief—in contrast to that of an appeal to
legislative or administrative bodies—is a principal induce-
ment to go to court.

The setting of such cases also minimizes the usual fear
of cranks' impeding important projects. In a hearing on an
application for preliminary relief, the court must make
an informed, though tentative, judgment both as to the
significance of the interests alleged to be at stake and as
to the likelihood that the plaintiffs might prevail on the
merits—that is, whether they have a legal claim that is not
frivolous. The proceeding for preliminary relief thereby
provides an expeditious screening process. If the judge
thinks the claim lacks merit, he can refuse to grant immediate relief; ordinarily this will be the end of the matter.
Or he may try to find some acceptable accommodation of
the parties' positions pending an opportunity to consider
the case in detail, so that the interests of all are protected

temporarily and informally. A judge might, for example, extract a promise from the defendant that he will not begin construction until notice is given the court and the plaintiff, particularly in a case where the plaintiff has been fearful of imminent action.

While limiting consideration of environmental litigation to such preliminary preventive cases largely mitigates the conventional fears of delays and cranks, it necessarily raises the question whether the delay problem is not simply shifted, rather than abated. In short, a defendant subject to a preliminary injunction is himself delayed and must withhold action until the legal issue is finally resolved, which may take some time. This, for example, has been the complaint of electric utility companies who fear that their long-range planning can be upset by injunctions granted at the behest of private citizens who may have what they view as extreme preservationist, antidevelopment views.

To this fear no absolute answer can be given which will satisfy everyone. Plainly, to allow any form of effective challenge is to take the risk that someone's plans or desires will be thwarted at least temporarily. This is a different form of delay than that which is usually charged against courts—that matters before them drag on interminably without meaningful resolution. As indicated above, that problem is not significantly presented by actions for immediate injunctive relief. Rather, the question is whether governmental or private-industry projects should be stopped at all. No satisfactory answer in theory can be given to this question. If one begins with the assumption that most plaintiffs are cranks and most projects unobjectionable, delay is obviously undesirable. Conversely, to the extent that delay is calculated to impose pressures for more adequate planning, which has been lacking, as in the Alaska pipeline case, delay seems a worthwhile investment indeed.

In considering this dilemma, though there is no completely satisfactory solution, the following facts are nonetheless significant. First, delay is never imposed simply because some dissatisfied citizen desires it. Only a judge can convert a plaintiff's desire for an injunction into an enforceable order. And judges, as noted above, do not simply grant injunctions because they are sought; they must be persuaded that important issues are at stake and that there is a reasonable likelihood of ultimate success by the plaintiff. Thus, agencies and industrial enterprisers who have carefully done their planning homework are in a very strong position to persuade a judge that no impediment should be placed in their way. Experience thus far with all the environmental cases litigated suggests very strongly that judges are most reluctant—as any sensible individual would be—to restrain important and extremely costly projects. They must be persuaded that something is wrong and that haste is undue.

The rather remarkable, but simple, fact is that in virtually every case where relief has been granted, the defendant could not adequately defend himself against even preliminary challenges. The Alaska pipeline case is a dramatic example of the usual situation. Had it been possible to persuade the judge that the statutory requirements had been met and that adequate studies had been made and implemented, plainly no injunction would have issued. But these showings could not be made, and the record made clear—as the material cited in the previous chapter shows—that the Interior Department did not act so as to justify the confidence which they demanded in asking for judicial deference. Indeed, the Interior Department's own documents said that the oil companies had "not demonstrated acceptable fundamental design criteria" for the pipeline they proposed to build and noted that "more consideration may have to be given to alternative routes." Despite this planning failure, government officials sought immediately to go forward with a permit for a road which was plainly designed to facilitate construction of the pipeline.

The granting of preliminary relief in such circumstances by a respected federal judge must never be confused with the notion of citizen-extremists on their own delaying important public projects. Conversely, it is perfectly clear that citizens who raise objections—whether right or wrong—will not move the courts to grant injunctive relief when they are unable to produce hard evidence of potential damage or of a need for delay. Many vigorous citizen-plaintiffs have learned this lesson to their dismay. As we shall see, if there is any one quality which predominantly characterizes the usual courtroom proceeding, it is judicial cautiousness.

All these protections against frivolous action and unjustifiable delay apply only to cases where preliminary injunctive relief is sought. Where does this leave those situations in which citizens might sue for money damages or for an order requiring remedial action? It leaves them, frankly, in the background.

Lawsuits seeking money damages for the public, by and large, are of secondary importance in environmental controversies. Most of the interests sought to be protected could not be easily compensated in damages in any event. Clean air and water for public use, scenic vistas, and the maintenance of fisheries and recreation areas, even where demonstrably harmed, rarely matter in significant dollar amounts to any particular identifiable citizen. The effects of environmental conditions are diffuse both in space and time, and rarely will a damage suit achieve the results sought. This is not to assert that such suits should be banned—only that they are not appropriately at the cutting edge of the movement for environmental quality. The prospect of damage suits may have some deterrent effect, but they tend to drag on interminably, with little result. Our attention need not be focused on them. Of course, damage suits brought by particular individuals who have suffered personal harm, such as those commonly brought by landowners against neighboring factories, will continue. Relief against such damage has always been available at law; it is only remedies sought on behalf of the community at large that is under inquiry here.

Demands for an order requiring a factory to clean up its wastes, or to ban harmful products, are important, for it is clear that many current environmental problems should be remedied. But lawsuits directed to this end, however commendable, are rarely effective. Except where a court can be persuaded that immediate relief is required, judges are reluctant to impose an immediate ban which in effect denies a defendant his right to a full hearing and appeal. Thus, and in contrast to injunctions against proposed action, such cases are amenable to problems of delay, protracted appeals, and debilitating legal warfare. For such situations the private lawsuit is generally an unsatisfactory tool.

Tactically, the environmental lawsuit is best employed as a preventive measure. In the large sense, too, it would seem desirable to focus attention on preventive action, and the litigation strategies discussed hereafter are designed to implement that point of view. Simply because courts cannot do everything well does not mean that they should be called upon to do nothing.

For other situations, other tactics will be better suited. The concept of effluent charges, for example, in which factories must pay certain fees as taxes for the wastes they emit, is a most promising means of dealing with conventional water and air pollution emission problems. Rather than judicial or administrative action taken to order certain waste control facilities to be built, it seems preferable to impose a relatively self-executing tax scheme which creates economic disincentives on waste-producing conduct. A similar sort of device might be imposed on many solid waste disposal problems; it is possible that junked automobiles as a problem might be dealt with by requiring manufacturers to reclaim and dispose of waste hulks, which would be simply another version of the effluent tax concept.

Still other problems may have to be dealt with by the imposition of specific prohibitory standards by legislation. Certain lands may have to be reserved for recreational or public uses. Certain products—detergents, pesticides, or nondegradable packages—may have to be outlawed or restricted. Scenic plots or parklands may have to be purchased.

These few examples only reemphasize the point made earlier that many routes will have to be attempted and many forms of leverage in all branches of government applied if we are to cope effectively with environmental quality problems. Preventive action, such as will be described, is one critical element in the solution of the environmental dilemma; to secure it, the courtroom is a most useful forum.

Finally, a word must be said about the fear that opening the judicial form is a two-edged sword that could be used as effectively by opponents of environmental quality as by its advocates or that new judicial remedies will create new opportunities for litigants to impede the work of progressive and effective public agencies as well as to challenge inadequate and slothful ones. Actually, that is not the issue at all—the issue is who has access to judicial remedies. Right now, today, the courtroom is widely available only to one class of potential litigants—those who claim that their private property rights are being impaired. Thus, individuals or industries subject to administrative agency orders requiring them to clean up pollution, to refrain from developing shoreline property, or to cease mining by destructive means or subject to other similar constraints are perfectly free to come into court and challenge such orders on the ground that they represent an infringement of property rights.

The problem now is that judicial remedies are essentially unequally available. One seeking to protect his private interests has full access to the courts. It is only those who seek relief on behalf of public rights, in their role simply as members of the public entitled to clean air and water and other such common resources, who have been denied the opportunity to obtain judicial intervention. Thus, progressive resource agencies are widely amenable to judicial attack, while the inadequate agencies—those who protect public rights too little—have alone had the right

to *prevent* judicial inquiry on the ground that they, and
they alone, are entitled to speak for the public. It is a
one-way street—what has brought us to our present position
is our traditional unwillingness to embrace some concept
of public, enforceable rights.

It is also said, though, that the present tradition of
broad judicial deference to administrative action, even
where that action cannot be said to infringe property
rights, protects "good" agency action from potentially
hostile judicial scrutiny. For example, a vigorous water
pollution control agency can theoretically impose more
rigorous standards than it could justify under judicial
scrutiny.

Such situations may arise, though one is hard pressed to
find many examples. Where they do exist, however, there
seems little reason to perpetuate them. No agency, however
noble its motives, ought to be permitted to regulate free
of scrutiny—if it cannot satisfy a skeptical judge of the
soundness of its decisions, it ought to have its decisions
overturned. An example of this problem arose not long
ago in Wisconsin.[1] A state agency had refused to grant a
town permission to fill land along the shoreline of a
river; when challenged by the town, the court held that
the agency's protective enthusiasm should not be allowed
to prevail in the absence of supporting evidence of potential

[1] Town of Ashwaubenon v. Public Service Commission, 22 Wis.2d 38,
125 N.W.2d 567 (1964). Naturally, a legislature might decide to impose
more rigorous judicial scrutiny over administrative action which allows
environmental disruption than over that which restrains it. In the former
case, for example, the risk of irreversible damage may be thought a grave
enough threat to the public interest to require thorough judicial reexamination. In the latter case, limited judicial review may be thought
adequate, it being recognized that a regulated party can always sue to
protect against regulation which amounts to expropriation of his property.

damage to the state's resources. It would not take the agency's decision upon faith nor find as a matter of law that no further development was permissible. Insofar as this sort of legal ruling impedes agency work by requiring them to obtain evidence which would support their judgment, such judicial intervention is all to the good.

It is said that to open up administrative action to a greater degree of judicial inquiry would encourage judges hostile to the work of the agencies to undermine their desirable regulatory functions. Unfortunately, judges hostile enough to any given activity can always find a way to subvert it. Only the naïve think the legal system so tight that it represses the strongly felt desires of determined men who stand at its helm. Legal rules can only open doors that law and tradition have kept fastened—they cannot, except in the grossest sense, make one walk through them.

Chapter 5

The Mind-Forged Manacles of Law

I

Environmental litigation is at a most uncertain state of development. In the years since 1965 considerable progress has been made toward recognizing the right of private citizens to sue and the amenability of government agencies to lawsuits. Both of these technical matters had for many years stood as virtually impregnable barriers against citizen-initiated cases.

Though it is now quite widely recognized that ordinary citizens have the right to complain about government misconduct through the initiation of lawsuits, there is a considerable degree of confusion and doubt about the issues which courts may examine once the citizen is permitted to come before them.

Thus far, courts have approached environmental cases very cautiously. For example, if citizens sue a highway agency on the ground that a proposed new road will have an unreasonable adverse impact on open space, on fish and wildlife, and on rivers that the road is to cross, it is most unlikely today that a court would decide the merits of such a claim in any direct sense. Rather, the judge would be likely to say that he can enjoin the highway department only in one of the following two instances: if they have violated some express provision of a statute or if they have acted "arbitrarily and capriciously, or without substantial evidence" to support their decision, as statutes often are phrased. These conventional constraints upon the role of the judiciary—a product of the grip which the administrative approach now has upon the governmental process—have seriously retarded and distorted the proper role of the courts in dealing with environmental disputes. Before examining the directions in which we must go henceforth, it is necessary first to understand where we stand today in regard to environmental litigation, and thereby to see how much we are still the captive of those administrative failures discussed earlier.

II

Violation of Statute. If there were a law prohibiting a highway agency from taking a right-of-way more than fifty feet wide, but the agency had condemned a hundred-foot wide swath for its project, a court would routinely enter an injunction against such illegality. Similarly, if a statute required the agency to hold public hearings or to obtain the views of the state conservation department, and they had failed to do so, an order would be entered prohibiting further action on the road until and unless those obligations had been fulfilled. These are the common situations of illegality with which courts are prepared to deal.

While such decisions result in the relief the plaintiffs desire—an injunction against further action—cases predicated on such claims have several severe disadvantages.

Obviously they make the opportunity for relief dependent upon the presence or absence of some legal standard which may have nothing whatever to do with the issue the parties actually seek to raise. The statute books are full of old, often obsolete, laws that it is in no one's interest vigorously to enforce. Naturally judges feel constrained to enforce plain legal rules that are brought to their attention, with the result that important projects may be needlessly delayed. At the same time, projects which deserve to be challenged may go forward simply because there is no general law which permits the real merits of the case to be litigated, and no such collateral matter as a right-of-way statute can be found. This situation promotes bad law and inconsistent and unforeseeable decisions, and it imposes upon lawyers an incentive to search the statute books for some legal peg—however dubious—upon which their client's interest can be vindicated.

The problem reached an ultimate of sorts when the Hudson River Expressway controversy, discussed in Chapter 3, went to court. Under the old Rivers and Harbors Law of 1899, it was provided that congressional approval had to be obtained when certain facilities such as bridges, dikes, and causeways were built in navigable waters. In 1946 Congress sensibly decided that it was wasting its time in enacting a statute whenever a structure such as a bridge had to be built, since in practice it simply accepted the opinions of agency engineers on the technical questions involved, and eventually authority to approve bridges and causeways was transferred to the appropriate federal departments.

For reasons that were never made clear, and which in all probability were nothing more than an oversight, responsibility for the authorization of dikes was never yielded by the Congress. Thus, as of 1968, when the Hudson River Expressway case came to court, it was still provided in the relevant statutes—in this case, the 1899 Rivers and Harbors Law—that no dike could be built in navigable waters without the express consent of Congress. If this retention of congressional authority over dikes was intentional, that intent was one of the best-kept secrets of legislative history—in all the changes which were made in the statutes, nobody ever said anything about dike-building one way or the other. It is not easy to identify any rationale for keeping this particular authority in the Congress. It hardly seems possible that in 1946 Congress secretly thought to itself that it had better keep its power over dikes to protect fish and wildlife. Moreover, federal officials say that in practice—at least until the expressway controversy arose—they rarely if ever bothered to obtain congressional authority when dikes were to be built,

All this intricate concern with obscure legislative enactments would be preposterously tiresome if it were not for the fact that in 1968 Judge Thomas Murphy of the U.S. District Court enjoined the Army Corps of Engineers from going forward with the Hudson River Expressway *on the express ground* that there was no Act of Congress authorizing the building of a dike in the Hudson that was to be filled and then covered with a road.[1]

Not only was this the holding of the court, but both plaintiff and defendant, in endless testimony and briefs, argued about whether the planned structure was a "dike" or should be called by some other name that would not

[1] Citizens Committee for the Hudson Valley *et al* v. Volpe *et al*, 302 F. Supp. 1083 (S.D.N.Y. 1969), aff'd. 425F.2d 97 (2d Cir. 1970).

have invoked the congressional-consent provision of the 1899 statute.

It may be hard to believe that this was what occupied lawyers and the judge in a case that consumed thirty trial days and produced a four-thousand page transcript, but it really happened. To be sure, as a literal reading of the statute, Judge Murphy was correct. The law *does* say that dikes cannot be built without an authorizing Act of Congress; the proponents of the expressway had—despite their later protestations—been calling the proposed structure a "dike"; and what they intended to build did meet the technical definition of a dike.

What makes all this so nonsensical, of course, is that the ability to obtain a court injunction against a project of this magnitude depended on whether or not a dike were being built—which was, of course, beside the point. Obviously, a riverfront expressway could technically be built on a structure not a dike, though it might raise the same fish-and-wildlife problems as the structure in the expressway case. Similarly, the mere presence of a dike does not itself demonstrate that there will be serious fish-and-wildlife problems, though that is what the case was really all about. And, most importantly, it is perfectly clear that the 1899 statute referring to dikes was passed at a time when Congress did not have the slightest inkling that it was interposing itself to protect the public against depredations of such natural habitat. The result in the case was utterly fortuitous. Many other projects are under consideration, where there are also serious fish-and-wildlife problems but where there is no dike and therefore no such legal basis for returning the matter to Congress.

It may well be that Judge Murphy was concerned about

this particular project on the merits and reached out to grasp a statutory straw to support his doing what he wanted to do. If that was the case, it would have been much better to say directly what he meant—if courts are going to dig into the merits of such cases, they ought to do so openly. At least then concerned lawyers could help to work out appropriate rules for approaching such matters. Moreover, there would then be an opportunity to invoke judicial relief whenever the problems of the expressway case were presented, whether or not a dike happened to be involved.

Conversely, it was possible that the judge was simply applying the law in a literal fashion, without any concern at all for the underlying issues and importance of the case. If that was so, the law proved to be an incredibly rigorous and wasteful institution in circumstances where there were more important issues to command judicial time and attention. In this respect, it should be remarked that nothing really compelled Judge Murphy to take the position he did. Another judge, who heard the case at an earlier stage on a motion for preliminary relief, interpreted the 1899 law as calling for congressional authority only when a dike presented the prospect of a substantial interference with navigation.[2] While the statute does not say that in so many words, it is an interpretation frankly more in keeping with an attempt to conform to congressional desires as of 1899.

We are entitled to expect more of the judiciary than what the Expressway case produced, yet this is characteristic of the present judicial approach to environmental litigation.

---

[2] 297 F. Supp. 804 (1969).

III

Procedural Failings. The other principal form of illegal conduct to which courts are prepared to respond is the failure to employ procedures required by law, such as the holding of a hearing, making studies or reports, consulting with other agencies, or taking evidence on all the issues upon which a decision ought to be based. Cases of this sort comprise the great bulk of environmental litigation to date. This is hardly surprising, for in the ever expanding and elaborate procedures that the legislatures impose upon administrative agencies, it is usually rather easy to find some procedural blunder or failing that can be called to the attention of a court. Moreover, cases of this kind give the courts an easy way out—without having to enmesh themselves in the merits of the dispute, they can simply require that all statutory procedures be followed and send the case back to the agency with an order that it hold new hearings, take additional evidence, or file required reports.

The famous Scenic Hudson case[3] is the preeminent example of this approach. Citizen groups objected to the plan of metropolitan New York's electric utility company, Consolidated Edison, to build a so-called "pumped-storage plant" on the Hudson River at Storm King Mountain, near the U.S. Military Academy at West Point. A pumped-storage plant is simply a sort of giant water-power storage battery, in which water is pumped to a reservoir at the top of a hill during times of day when the system has

[3] Scenic Hudson Preservation Conference v. Federal Power Commission, 354 F.2d 608 (2d Cir. 1965), cert. denied 384 U.S. 941 (1966).

excess generating capacity, to be released for the generation of power during times when the system has high demand.

In the Scenic Hudson case, it was asserted by citizen objectors that the proposed plant would have an adverse effect on the scenic values of the area, as well as on fish and resources in the river, because of the alternate pumping and releasing of great amounts of water. It was charged that the Federal Power Commission, which had licensing authority over the project, had not adequately considered the potential effects on conservation of natural resources and scenic and historic preservation and that it had failed adequately to consider alternative means of providing needed electric power.

The court agreed, and in a strongly worded opinion, criticized the Commission for acting

> as an umpire blandly calling balls and strikes for adversaries appearing before it; the right of the public must receive active and affirmative protection at the hands of the Commission . . . The Commission must see to it that the record is complete. . . . Renewed proceedings must include as a basic concern the preservation of natural beauty and of national historic shrines, keeping in mind that, in our affluent society, the cost of a project is only one of several factors to be considered.

With this, the court returned the matter to the Commission for further proceedings. The remanded hearing consumed 72 days and produced a transcript of more than 12,000 pages with some 350 extensive exhibits. Four years later, to the surprise of no one, the Commission's hearing examiner again recommended that the license be issued.

In August 1970, the Commission finally issued a decision approving the project, but the controversy is still far from ended.

The history of the Scenic Hudson case is by no means unusual. Indeed, it is the rare exception in which a judicial remand to an administrative agency for further procedures results in a changed decision. The reason may be found if we ponder the implications of cases like Hunting Creek and the Hudson River Expressway—it is not lack of information or evidence that principally infects the administrative process, but the perspectives and attitudes that the administrators bring to the problems set before them.

One need only look at the hearing examiner's report in the Scenic Hudson case, issued in August 1969 following the extensive remanded proceedings, to get a sense of impact on him of all the elaborate evidence submitted. The examiner brushed aside the question of electric generation capacity actually required—an issue upon which testimony running into thousands of pages was adduced by the objectors—with the bland observation that acceptance of the citizens' proposals "would constitute an unwarranted invasion of an area very properly to be left to the reasonable discretion of management."

On another question, he said "the suggestion runs counter to accepted public utility cost concepts and is rejected." Evidence on the important issue of interconnection with other utility systems as a source of reserve electric capacity was disregarded because, the examiner held, it "will depend upon developments on other systems which cannot now be entirely foreseen." And the testimony of a principal witness was dismissed with the following comment: "Exhibiting little knowledge of area growth and reserves . . . his generalized observations are of no value as leading to useful findings and conclusions."

The tone of such opinions and the attitude they convey tell us, as they should tell the courts, how little administrative decisions usually depend upon such issues as the amplitude of an evidentiary record or the fulfillment of public hearing requirements, to which the courts have thus far so largely devoted their efforts in the realm of supervision of administrative action. From time to time, the administrative perspective is so baldly exhibited that even the most restrained members of the judiciary feel called upon to speak bluntly. Chief Justice Warren E. Burger, while still a member of the U.S. Court of Appeals, said of a decision by a Federal Communications Commission examiner something that might aptly be applied to decisions such as that in the Scenic Hudson case and others of its kind. The decision exhibited, he said,[4]

a curious neutrality-in-favor-of-the-licensee. . . . To borrow a phrase from the Examiner, his response manifests a "glaring weakness" in his grasp of the function and purpose of the hearing and the public duties of the Commission. . . . The entire hearing was permeated by . . . the pervasive impatience—if not hostility—of the Examiner, a constant factor which made fair and impartial consideration impossible. . . . As we view the record the Examiner tended to impede the exploration of the very issues which we would reasonably expect the Commission itself would have initiated; an ally was

[4] Office of Communication, United Church of Christ v. Federal Communications Commission, 425F.2d 543 (D.C. Cir. 1969).

regarded as an opponent. . . . The Examiner and the Commission exhibited at best a reluctant tolerance of this court's mandate and at worst a profound hostility to the participation of the Public Intervenors and their efforts.

The difficulty with litigation in which courts limit themselves to a correction of legal failings of the kind indicated by the Hudson River Expressway case, with its concern about an eighty-year-old "dike" law, or the Scenic Hudson case, with its remand for correction of procedural failings, is that it fails to focus upon the real underlying problem— the attitude, rather than the legality, of administrative action. The significant potential strength of the judiciary in correcting environmental misconduct is sapped because courts hesitate to inquire into the merits, rather than the peripheral legalities, of environmental issues.

A theory and mechanism for implementing enforceable public rights remain to be developed. Without them, the result is haphazard instances in which delay of questionable projects can be obtained, depending on the presence or absence of some more or less relevant statute that can be called into operation—and often unnecessary delay of proposed action, without the true merits of the controversy ever being considered—while cases are sent back again and again for more administrative fiddling, consuming years of time and scarce resources of money and manpower to make gigantic, and usually pointless, amplified records before some bureaucratic tribunal.

Perhaps most disturbing, such cases promote a disingenuity on the part of both lawyers and the courts. It is clear to everyone that cases of the kind described in this chapter, though they purport to be literal applications of specific legal rules, imply some evaluation by the courts that the challenged project is, on its merits, dubious at best and that some delay is not going to do any harm. A court persuaded that the pumped-storage plant must be built, or that the Hudson River Expressway and the Alaska pipeline are urgent necessities, could always find a way to circumvent apparent failure to comply with the statutes. So these cases represent a mixture of traditional constrained judicial review and a reaching out to do something about important environmental issues that are not otherwise being adequately dealt with. The result is a distortion of that directness and candor which characterizes any rational governmental process and a realization of the old lawyer's saying that "hard cases make bad law."

IV

Arbitrary and Capricious Action. It was said at the beginning of this chapter that in addition to judicial review of the compliance of administrative agencies with express statutory mandates, courts also traditionally reviewed administrative action to determine whether it is arbitrary or capricious or unsupported by evidence. In theory such review is much less tightly constrained than mere enforcement of statutory requirements, but in fact this aspect of judicial review has rarely provided much scope for court action. In most instances, a highway commission or other such agency that follows standard engineering practices and that can produce conventional reports from its engineers and contractors supporting the proposed action will be allowed to prevail against citizen challenge.

Ironically, then, the very issue which citizens seek to raise in environmental cases—the inadequacy of conventional engineering practices—is insulated from judicial attack by a defense indicating that the agency acted conventionally and thus not "arbitrarily or capriciously."

In a typical, well-known highway case,[5] for example, the judge was very critical of the highway department and particularly of its assertion—in the face of concerted local opposition—that the proposed road would enhance the areas through which it was to pass. The affected people in the community, the judge commented, might well view this conclusion as "so bizarre to be almost irrational." Nonetheless, he said, the opponents did not make out a case of arbitrariness or caprice. As an engineering matter, the route chosen was "the correct choice," he observed, "It is shorter, straighter and cheaper." He concluded: "I cannot say that the Administrator's evaluation of the evidence was contrary to its overwhelming weight. . . . The decision must be allowed to stand unless it was plainly wrong. . . . I conclude that this administrative decision was not wrong enough to permit this court to upset it."

Other cases demonstrate the usual limitations of judicial action even more explicitly. In a suit challenging the U.S. Forest Service,[6] the judge said that for the plaintiff citizens to prevail,

[it] must appear that the action of the agency was in effect malicious and illegal, and the principle of arbitrary action is not applicable if the action was a rational action resulting from a consideration of the factors involved.

[5] Road Review League v. Boyd, 270 F.Supp. 650 (S.D.N.Y. 1967).

[6] Gandt v. Hardin, Civil Action No. 928-70 (U.S. Dist. Ct., W.D. Mich., Dec. 11, 1969, Judge W. Wallace Kent).

. . . The burden of proof in connection with an action such as this is completely upon the plaintiffs. They can only prevail if they can establish by clear and convincing proof that the action of the defendants is arbitrary and capricious and not in accordance with law.

Obviously a burden such as this on the plaintiff is at best difficult to carry, for administrators do not act irrationally in the sense that they build highways to nowhere or permit hot-dog vendors to sell their wares on the White House lawn. The essential point of environmental litigation is not to establish that bureaucrats should be consigned to lunatic asylums, but to prove that they often fail to consider and act upon evidence of proposed environmental damage—evidence of a kind that has not been a part of traditional decision-making and should now be considered in the regulatory and administrative process. Thus it is the claim that they have failed to do something which ought to be done, rather than that they have done their traditional work irrationally, that is sought to be brought into question.

The failure of courts generally to respond to this demand for a new and enlarged perspective cuts the heart out of the environmental lawsuit before it can even begin. The inadequacy of this traditional judicial approach can also be best illustrated by reference to a highway location dispute. Citizens in New Jersey objected to a proposed new segment of the interstate highway system which was to pass through or near their communities.[7] They pointed to potential adverse effects on the area, to which they

[7] Township of Hopewell v. Goldberg, 101 N.J. Super. 589, 245 A.2d 67, *cert.* denied 52 N.J. 500, 246 A.2d 457 (1968).

said the highway department had given inadequate attention. In addition, they took upon themselves the initiative of hiring a distinguished highway planner, Ian McHarg, to prepare and present an alternative scheme which they said considered and met the issues of proposed environmental damage.

The citizens claimed, not unreasonably, that their proposal should be measured against the official highway department plan, and if the evidence demonstrated their plan to be feasible and less damaging, the highway department ought to be enjoined from continuing with its proposal. Thus they sought to enforce a claimed right to environmentally sound planning, and they stood ready to support that claim with evidence. Parenthetically it should be noted that they first sought to persuade highway officials themselves in the usual long process of public hearings, but their efforts were brushed aside with the same sort of arrogant disregard which we have already seen in abundance.

So the citizens came to court, where they were met with the usual stifling assertion that they must prove arbitrariness or caprice. The court refused to consider the highway-routing question on its merits. It simply asked whether the highway department had carried out the formal functions that the law imposed upon it. Approaching the question quantitatively, the court found

that the requirements for public hearings, and notice thereof, were substantially met; that the local needs were considered; that appropriate local officials were consulted; that economic effects were considered; alternate routes studied and an opportunity to express objections to the proposed route given. The record shows that the proposed route alignment was given lengthy study and consideration.

The court thus concluded that all the proper procedures had been followed, though it evinced no interest in the quality or nature of those proceedings. Form the law required, and form it had. In addition, since the plaintiffs had raised the question of arbitrary and capricious action, the court said it must inquire whether "there is substantial credible evidence present in the record to support the proposed route alignment." On this issue, the court held that the law was satisfied because the highway department, following standard practices, had selected a route that, conforming with those practices, was appropriate according to the evidence the highway department chose to present. In other words, the highway department wins so long as it plays the game by its own rules. Perhaps there is nothing arbitrary or capricious in this procedure; but it bypasses the central question which such suits seek to raise—the ability of the highway department to justify, on the merits, the consistency of its plan with a concern for the preservation of environmental quality and to withstand comparison with the alternate plan advanced by the plaintiffs.

In refusing to entertain this central question, the court relied upon the old saw, "our function is not to substitute our judgment for that of the [Highway] Commissioner even if we should disagree with his determination," when it should have been perfectly obvious that the plaintiffs did not want a resolution of the controversy representing the judge's judgment about highway planning—they wanted a forum in which to present evidence and a judge who would hear evidence and determine whether the Commissioner's decision could be supported when tested against the challenge of other experts and other alternatives presented. What they got was a decision as to whether the evidence that the highway department chose to present as *its* record seemed arbitrary when measured against its conclusion. The citizens got, in essence, the back of the judicial hand, indicating the impertinence of their seeking to challenge the expertise of the "experts."

Lest it be thought that citizen plaintiffs in cases such as this are asking the impossible of the courts or seeking to convert judges into amateur highway engineers, it is instructive to look for a moment at the issue that the New Jersey citizens' case actually sought to put before the court.

The highway being challenged was a proposed thirty-mile segment of Interstate 95, running north and south through New Jersey. The essence of the complaint of local people, first raised in a series of public hearings, was that the route would bisect established communities and cut unnecessarily through important natural areas. Alternatives along established highways and railroad rights-of-way or another less disruptive corridor to the west were suggested.

The highway department's route was not its own first choice. It had wanted a westerly route, but it could not get federal approval for that more expensive corridor. Its second choice, the disputed route, was selected as one part of a projected alternative to the New Jersey Turnpike. Authority had not been obtained to build the whole through-route, however, and so the proposed segment paralleled the existing Turnpike for some distance and was then to feed back into it.

The details of the various proposals are unimportant here—the point is simply that in the I-95 controversy, as in many other disputes over the federal interstate highway system, it seemed that a highway was being built at least in significant part simply because the federal highway trust fund was there as a source of financing. State highway officials, unable to get enough money to build the most desirable route, would nonetheless be loath to turn away money available to build something, and so a second or third choice compromise was selected.

The highway department's public hearings were lively and well attended, and they made clear the issues that the citizens wished to raise, and that ultimately brought them into the courtroom. One citizen suggested that since this was to be an interstate highway for long-distance travel, people should not mind going a few miles further to reach established highway areas. The answer he got was that studies showed that eighty-five percent of traffic utilizing the proposed highway would be local. One might have assumed from this that the highway was being built to meet a present local demand in the proposed corridor. But when someone else at another point asked why they did not plan to build the corridor to the east, near existing Route 1, she was told that the "corrdior was changed because in the study of the trend of development, the trend was toward the west," where the highway was to be built. Apparently, she was to be satisfied with the explanation that the road was being built in anticipation of *future* demand. It did not occur to the highway representative to comment on the possibility that the "trend of development" might itself follow, and be largely influenced by, the presence of highways. Nor did he explain why, if the highway was to be built for local use, the overwhelming local opposition was not a most powerful factor indeed.

When the woman asked why the highway could not be routed even further west, thus skirting existing communities, the only answer she got was that such a route "would have taken us [to] the next corridor in the future to be developed." Why that modest change would be inappropriate, even though it was in the "next" corridor, was never explained either as to cost, distance, or projected demand. The issue was a particularly relevant one, for the state highway commissioner himself, only a few months earlier, had said: "[As] a matter of fact, we were hopeful that the route could be much west of its present intended general alignment, hoping we could open up new corridors." That hope had apparently been frustrated by the limitation of currently available federal funds. At this point, the beleagured lady said, "I guess I give up. Thank you."

The local people involved in the I-95 dispute, more sophisticated than many, knew that they could not come unprepared to a crowded public hearing room and hope to prevail on haphazard objections. They therefore did a very sensible thing: as noted earlier, they hired Ian McHarg to prepare an alternative route that would meet the reasonable needs of the highway builders and at the same time minimize the adverse impacts of the state's proposal on their communities.

McHarg worked out an ingenious scheme for determining the most appropriate routing for such a highway:[8]

> In essence, the method consists of identifying the area
> of concern as consisting of certain processes, in land,
> water and air—which represent values. These can be
> ranked—the most valuable land and the least, the
> most valuable water resources and the least, the most
> and least productive agricultural land, the richest wild-
> life habitats and those of no value, the areas of great and
> little scenic beauty, historic buildings and their absence
> and so on. The interjection of a highway will transect
> this area; it will destroy certain values. Where will it
> destroy the least? Positively the highway requires cer-
> tain conditions—propitious slopes, good foundation
> materials, rock, sand and gravel for its construction and
> other factors. Propitious circumstances represent savings,
> adverse factors are costs. Moreover, the highway can be
> consciously located to produce new values—more in-
> tense and productive land uses adjacent to intersections,
> a delightful experience for the motorist, an added con-
> venience to the traveler. The method requires that we
> obtain the most benefit for the least cost but that we
> include as values social process, natural resources and
> beauty.

We can identify the critical factors affecting the physical construction of a highway and rank these from least
to greatest cost. We can identify social values and rank

8 Ian McHarg: *Design with Nature* (New York: Natural History Press;
1969), p. 34; see also the comprehensive study prepared for the I-95 dis-
pute, in which the approach set out here was first developed, by Wallace,
McHarg, Roberts & Todd, Architects and Regional Planners: *Highway
Route Selection Method—Applied to I-95 Between the Delaware and
Raritan Rivers, New Jersey* (n.d.).

them from high to low. Physiographic obstructions—the need for structures, poor foundations, etc.—will incur high social costs. We can represent these identically. For instance, let us map physiographic factors so that the darker the tone, the greater the cost. Let us similarly map social values so that the darker the tone, the higher the value. Let us make the maps transparent. When these are superimposed, the least-social-cost areas are revealed by the lightest tone.

The scheme was, of course, simply a graphic representation of what any highway department should be doing when they take into account the many facts which they are supposed to consider in laying out a highway route. If, in this case, their considerations had been essentially the same as McHarg's, their route would have closely paralleled his.

In fact, however, the McHarg scheme included factors which were slighted in the highway department's planning—and, significantly, they are factors which are now supposed to play an important role in highway-planning. In essence, the highway department analysis was a study of traffic facilitation and patterns of urbanization—a classic highway-engineering approach, with some accommodation to skirt specific facilities such as parks. McHarg focused on a range of existing natural values and attempted to route a highway to insure the maintenance and enhancement of those values.

Only in a setting such as this does the idea of differing perspectives take on meaning and substance and present an opportunity to make real and important policy choices. Given no obvious choice such as is presented by maps and studies underlying them, the multidimensional nature of highway building remains empty rhetoric, glossed over by judicial opinions. And those opinions treat as a fact to be believed rather than an assertion to be tested the statement of a highway department that it has amply considered all relevant alternatives.

No one, of course, would suggest that simply because a consultant has prepared an alternative route, it ought *ipso facto* to be accepted, any more than the highway department's plan ought to be accepted on blind faith. Rather, the presentation of such an outside consultant's proposal should be utilized as an opportunity to examine the question whether—as statutes now are beginning to demand—all reasonable and feasible alternatives for the maintenance of natural values are being considered and implemented by administrative agencies.

Instead, what the citizens of New Jersey got for their trouble—for their efforts to participate responsibly in a decision which significantly affected them—was a facile dismissal of the McHarg proposal by the highway department's engineering consultants and by the court.

V

Instances such as the New Jersey highway case suggest that "arbitrariness and caprice" or illegality in the traditional sense is not really the issue; moreover, they make clear that neither is the issue one of technical expertise beyond the competence of a judge or a legislator. A comparison of the McHarg proposal and the highway department proposal makes it clear that the critical issue was a policy choice, not an arcane matter of engineering.

What the plaintiffs in the New Jersey case desired was the opportunity to show that important, legislatively-recognized public policy considerations had been insufficiently regarded by the highway department and that an alternative scheme, technically and economically feasible and incorporating those public policies, could have been substituted. They asked only for the opportunity to be allowed to submit testimony in support of their claim and to prevail in the lawsuit if they could satisfy the judge that they were correct.

To be sure, if testimony had indicated to the judge that the proposed alternative did not show, by adequate evidence, engineering feasibility or if there had been an unresolved conflict of some other technical nature, no one would have expected the court to resolve the matter. The judge's job is only to weigh the evidence presented and to determine whether the party who bears the burden of proof has fulfilled it. It was this determination that was denied the plaintiffs in the New Jersey case—and that denial was important because it implied a judicial failure to recognize the citizens' right, enforceable by law, to environmentally sound planning. It is this right that is the essence of a true law of the environment—that provides a true opportunity for citizens to have a meaningful role in the determination of their environmental future.

Today that right is nowhere recognized nor enforced except in the most haphazard and irregular fashion. The courts are not to be blamed; indeed, they have in many instances gone out of their way to give needed relief in practice, if not in theory, as decisions such as that in the Hudson River Expressway case indicate. Many courts have become sensitive to the problem but feel constrained by the absence of a theory of citizens' rights to environmental quality and by a concern that courts are not equipped to adjudicate those rights. They are locked in by traditional notions of the limited scope of judicial review of administrative action, feeling—wrongly—that special deference must be paid to administrative expertise when they are, in fact, usually only giving the courts' imprimatur to administrative politics.

Two tasks thus face the legal system. The first is to begin identifying the nature of public rights in matters pertaining to environmental quality; the second is to help courts see their way toward a liberation from the administrative-review syndrome of crabbed inquiries such as have been noted in the preceding pages of this chapter.

Public rights to environmental quality must begin to be viewed in a fashion similar to private rights—to be seen as capable of direct evaluation on their merits within the framework of the common-law system and freed from excessive deference to the decisions, and the records made, by administrative officials. In short, public rights must be removed from the stranglehold which bureaucrats now have upon them and returned to their true "owners"—citizens *as* members of the public.

A few halting steps have already been taken in this direction, and some ancient concepts of the law can and should be revived and restored to help facilitate that process. The next chapters are dedicated to an exploration of the means for achieving this task.

Chapter 6

The Court
as Catalyst

If every state were to pass a law making clear that courts should consider the merits of citizen-initiated environmental cases, part of the problem considered in the preceding chapter would be mitigated—that is, judges and attorneys would not feel compelled to twist the questions that the litigants are actually trying to raise into such traditional issues as a claim of arbitrariness or a failure to comply with some explicit statutory command such as how a dike must be authorized or how wide a highway right-of-way may be.

Even if these constraints were to be removed, a serious problem would remain, for neither judges nor attorneys clearly see the nature of the governmental problem with which they are faced. As indicated earlier, two questions particularly trouble them. First, courts fear that if they embark upon a consideration of the "merits" of environmental disputes, they will be taking upon themselves a primary role in public policy-making which they feel—with justification—should reside in the legislative branch of government. Second, judges are troubled about their competence to decide what seem to be highly technical issues—how much radiation can a nuclear plant safely emit, how fragile is the Alaskan tundra, how sensitive are fish to hot water discharges in a river?

Of these two concerns, the question of judicial competence is disposed of most easily. Courts are never asked to resolve technical questions—they are only asked to determine whether a party appearing before them has effectively borne the burden of proving that which he asserts. Thus the question is not one of substituting judicial knowledge for that of experts, but whether a judge is sufficiently capable of understanding the evidence put forward by expert witnesses to decide whether the party who has the burden of proof has adduced evidence adequate to support his conclusion.

Why this question has seemed particularly troublesome in this context of environmental litigation is rather perplexing—courts are called upon frequently to decide cases in which the evidence of technical experts is crucial. Medical malpractice, product safety, and industrial accident cases, to take only a few examples, are routine grist for the judicial mill. Indeed, the very issues that arise in environmental cases of the type discussed in this book are today subject to judicial inquiry if they arise in a slightly different context. For example, if an oil spill such as occurred at Santa Barbara gave rise to a suit for damages after the fact, courts would have to decide whether the oil drilling had been carried out in a reasonably safe fashion. Similarly, if an accident occurred at a power plant and suit were brought to recover damages, a court would have to decide whether the plant had been adequately constructed and operated.

The sort of environmental litigation proposed here simply shifts the questions involved forward in time. Rather than deciding the issue of reasonable precautions against the risk of harm retrospectively, the courts will be asked to decide those questions prospectively. To be sure, we know less about risks before they occur, but that does not change the legal issues involved—in a damage case for harm done, the question is what precautions the defendant should have taken in advance to avoid risks of harm that might reasonably have been foreseen. The question is thus always what should have been known before action was taken—and this is exactly the issue in environmental crises.

In short, the question of judicial competence is a false issue, a red herring. The case studies presented in Chapters 8 and 9 and particularly in Chapter 10 indicate specifically the ability of courts to cope with the merits of environmental litigation. They will speak for themselves on the question of judicial competence.

Far more important is the issue of judicial infringement of legislative policy-making, for most environmental litigation turns not on technical issues, but on disputes over policy, as the cases discussed in this book demonstrate. If there is any significant issue to be raised about environmental lawsuits, it is their impact on the legislative policy-making function. Here one reaches the central point about environmental litigation: the role of courts is not to make public policy, but to help assure that public policy is made by the appropriate entity, rationally and in accord with the aspirations of the democratic process.

The job of courts is to raise important policy questions in a context where they can be given the attention they deserve and to restrain essentially irrevocable decisions until those policy questions can be adequately resolved.

The New Jersey highway dispute, discussed in the preceding chapter, neatly exemplifies this distinction. It was said there that the court should have considered the plaintiffs' testimony regarding an alternative plan to that of the highway department and should have enjoined the highway department if the court found that the weight of evidence established inconsistencies between the highway department proposal and an intelligent highway policy or found existing highway policy unmet by the highway department plan.

Nothing in such a case suggests that the court should usurp the legislative role in formulating highway policy. At most, it asks one of two things: (1) The court should test the existing official plan against policies already articulated (more or less specifically in the law) and withhold approval of a proposal that is at odds with the policy or raises serious doubts about its effectuation. Or (2), if the court finds the proposal at odds with an environmentally sound policy, though it may not now be expressed in any legislation, and it finds no urgency for immediate construction, it withholds approval until and unless the policy question is returned to the legislative forum for open and decisive action. As we shall see, the court can help to promote open and decisive action in the legislative forum in several ways. By enjoining conduct on the part of government or industry, it can thrust upon those interests with the best access to the legislature the burden of obtaining legislative action. Also, the very presence of a lawsuit and the information it reveals promote attention in the press, which serves to alert citizens that an issue is arising which deserves their attention. In this way, too, litigation helps to realize a truly democratic process.

Notably, nothing in a case like the Interstate 95 controversy in New Jersey suggests that the courts ought to displace legislative judgment. The court serves either to implement an existing legislative policy against administrative disregard or to withhold irrevocable action until a policy can be considered and adequately formulated for action. To be sure, judges must make some tentative judgment about what the policy is, or should be—but the important reservation is the word "tentative." It is a judgment that is subject to—indeed, that encourages—legislative consideration, not one which displaces legislative consideration. Rather than being at odds with legislative policy-making, the courts are promoting that process and—at most—prodding it to operate with open consideration of important issues, and with an alerted public.

As we shall see in the pages which follow, this is a most important point, for the decisions which comprise the great bulk of environmental lawsuits are *not* decisions articulated by legislatures, but almost always decisions by administrators, usually at a rather low level in the hierarchy, employing their own discretion from their perspectives in the presence of vague and sometimes contradictory statutory policies. For this reason, paradoxical though it may seem, judicial intervention, rather than posing the threat of undermining the legislative function, actually operates to enhance it.

A most instructive example of this problem will be noted in Chapter 8. There a state highway department took parkland for a proposed highway right-of-way. Citizens sued and the highway department defense was that it was enforcing legislative policy to build highways. The citizen plaintiffs said the highway department was undermining other legislative policies in favor of saving parks. The dispute—an important issue of policy choice, which no statute clearly resolved as to a given highway condemnation case—was brought to court. The court found that a serious question was raised about the balance between roads and parks, found that the highway department was deciding the policy question for itself in favor of roads, and sent the case back to the legislature for action and clarification.

To understand that the principal role of courts is to raise important policy questions is to understand as well the fear that judicial intervention will interfere with large-scale long-term planning. As noted earlier, environmental litigation does not ask of a judge that he devise national policy nor that he repeal any settled statutory policy in contravention of explicit legislative desires. Rather, by inquiring into the effects of such policies in individual instances, it asks the courts to help promote the sort of continuous review and reevaluation that any large-scale program needs—and that legislatures often find themselves without time or adequate initiatives to undertake on a regular basis.

Again, the federal highway program provides a useful example. Plainly, there is a large federal transportation policy embodied in the highway program. It is, however, a policy that is necessarily implemented over a long period of time and hence eminently deserving of periodic reconsideration. Presumably, as the program goes forward, we learn some things and want to rethink some of our earlier assumptions about the program. The courts help Congress and state legislatures to do this, both in the large and the small sense.

In the smaller sense, courts can call attention to the impact of the highway program on parklands or on housing and can send highway agencies back to the legislatures both to get more detailed policy statements about the costs they are willing to incur to promote the program and to educate the legislatures from time to time on what those costs are. In this respect the courts serve to gather and feed useful information back into the legislative policy process, which, it must be emphasized, must be continuous if it is to be at all rational.

In the larger sense, judicial injunctions against various elements of the highway program, on the ground that they infringe other national policies or do unseemly harm, promote a search for better alternatives or new technologies.

One only understands this if he begins to see planning as something more than a legislative commitment once made to spend a lot of money, which is never to be reexamined or requestioned over the years and decades that follow. Only if we could be persuaded that every large project—whether governmental or private—was perfectly conceived at the outset, impregnable to new facts or new public concerns, and perfectly executed, could we view litigation as an infringement of planning and large-scale social policy activities. That, of course, is the posture that challenged administrators and enterprisers take, but as the preceding chapters should have made clear, if we take them not on their assertions, but on the demonstrable facts, it is a position of the greatest possible dubiety. There may be no more needed public function today than a forum that can send some of our Big Planners back to the drawing boards.

One final comment should be made on the problem of judicial interference with established legislative policies. There is a pervasive notion that every statute on the books is to be treated as a pure and thoroughly considered embodiment of the legislative will. This is the way in which lawyers always talk, for example, when they are defending a statute as stating the "intent of Congress."

Not to put too fine a point on it, this is bunk. There are all kinds of laws, and any effort to deal intelligently with environmental or other serious problems must begin by moving away from this preposterous concept. Some laws do indeed represent the conclusion of a carefully considered, hard and openly fought legislative enterprise. The federal Wilderness Act, which will be discussed in Chapter 9, is an example of such a statute. This is not to say that it is a perfect law or one that does not reflect some considerable horse-trading, but only that the various interests had their say, fought it out, and got the most they could get, including a rather clear statement of national policy.

Many other laws cannot with any degree of honesty be so described. The state bill authorizing the conveyance of the lands at Hunting Creek in Virginia did not meet this test. It was essentially a one-man bill, enacted without hearings or publicity by a busy legislature unaware of the competing interests that would have defined the issues if the bill had been adequately considered. Indeed, once the issues had been defined, the legislature repealed the law; fortunately, other forces kept the project in abeyance until this happened.

The dike law in the 1899 Rivers and Harbors Act represents still another sort of flawed legislation. Though it was used in the Hudson River Expressway case in support of a good environmental cause, it would be fatuous to claim that its congressional assent provisions for dikes reflected any meaningful 1970's policy of the Congress of the United States. It is certainly not a Wilderness Act nor a National Labor Relations Act.

Plainly courts cannot, and should not, be asked to declare laws now on the books to be dead letters or to engage in judicial repeal. But courts can, and should, use their powers to forestall projects lacking a demonstrated imminency of need, which are justified on the basis of dubious legislation, in order to encourage the legislature to take another look, and perhaps a more careful and open one, at the policy problems resulting from the way in which such laws are being implemented.

Courts have many devices available that enable them to act in a discriminating fashion without taking on overtly the function of weighing the quality of various kinds of legislation. The courts may read a law very narrowly if they have doubt about the propriety of the policy it embodies, or about the manner in which it was passed. Or the courts may hold that some readings of a dubious law would raise constitutional questions, and they may interpret the law restrictively to avoid such issues. In each instance, the courts thrust upon the legislature the obligation to affirm openly its true intent. These devices are all well established and have been used in various settings. They deserve particular attention in the environmental area, where some bureaucrat may seize upon some provision in a statute in the name of the solemn intent and desire of the legislature.

In sum, the court serves as a catalyst, not a usurper, of the legislative process.

Chapter 7

The Public Trust: A New Charter of Environmental Rights

I

With some of the negative concerns about judicial action now behind us, we can begin to consider the affirmative function of courts. If courts are to move more vigorously toward protecting environmental quality, what meaning are they to read into that very broad and vague concept?

The answer to this question is not easy, but it is by no means as obscure as many people seem to think. It is fashionable today to talk about enacting laws which guarantee to every person the "right to a decent environment." By itself this phrase means little, but it suggests a most interesting approach to the problem—it implies that persons *have* rights simply by virtue of their status as members of the public and that those rights should be phrased in a way to put them on a plane with traditional private property rights.

The analogy to private property rights itself suggests the beginning of an answer: if one thinks about the basic law governing rights of private property in land, he finds those rights protected by the old legal maxim *sic utere tuo ut alienum non laedas*—use your own property in such a manner as not to injure that of another. While the maxim has sometimes been dismissed by scholars as mere question-begging verbiage, as a source of ideas about public rights to environmental quality it is most useful.

Simply because one owns a tract of land and has exclusive possession of its surface, he may not necessarily sponsor rock concerts or motorcycle races at midnight. The use of his land has spillover effects on the use of his neighbor's land, and so each must constrain his own desires to use and profit from his land in order to protect the ability of his neighbor to act in a like fashion.

The maxim thus states two principles that are relevant to the issue of public rights to environmental quality. First, even one's legitimate activity has spillover effects on the rights of others that limit its scope and nature. And second, the limit of one's rights is measured by the ability of his neighbor to make a reasonably productive use of his own property. While this formulation does not decide the details of individual cases, it tells one that he has a duty to take all reasonable steps to minimize the harm to his neighbor, who is entitled to enforce that duty.

The striking fact revealed by this little exercise in legal theory is that while it has provided a basis for resolving disputes among neighboring private property owners, under the rubric of the law of nuisance it has not been carried over to protect those important public interests which are not ordinarily the subjects of private ownership —such as the ambient air, water, open space, the seashore, and all the other resources which comprise the repositories of environmental quality.

It should not be understood by these comments that there is *no* legal protection for air, water, and open space;

rather the point is that there is no legal protection enforce-able *as a right by a citizen in his capacity as a member of the public.* And, having seen something of the limitations on protection of these rights at the hands of administrative middlemen in public agencies, the distinction must be viewed as a critical one.

If an individual comes into court to protest the government-approved construction or operation of a factory on the ground that it will degrade the ambient air to an unreasonable degree and asserts that he is entitled to protection against such degradation as a matter of legal right—the same right he would have to enforce against a neighbor keeping pigs in the backyard—he could turn to no body of law that would support such a claim. He does not have a legal right he may enforce under the *sic utere . . .* maxim, whereby he may get a court to consider the harm to him as a member of the public and hear evidence of the reasonable alternatives which would accommodate both his asserted right to environmental quality in clean air and the factory's asserted interest in producing its product. Quite the contrary, in most every state he would be thrown out of court and told that conduct affecting him solely as an individual citizen, in common with every other citizen, can be challenged only by public officials.

A central purpose of this book is to establish that he should have just such a right and that courts can enforce that right much as they enforce private property law. Indeed, if we could get the courts to adapt the nuisance concept to public rights in environmental quality, we would be far down the road toward coping with the problems of environmental quality.

Thus far, however, the law has been unwilling to recognize that citizens have such rights, that they are enforceable, and that they may be enforced against the government as well as against private parties. For government agencies, in issuing permits for oil-drilling, land-filling, timber-cutting, and factory construction, are often primarily responsible for permitting excessive environmental degradation.

There is no good reason why we should hesitate to adopt a theory of public rights to environmental quality, enforceable at law, nor is there any reason to think we cannot adjudicate the reasonable accommodations needed to protect against unnecessary threats to the environment. If the courts viewed the public interest in the Alaskan environment or the Hudson River as they do private property, they could go straight to the merits of the claims which citizens want to make. The same questions asked in private cases apply to public complaints: Is the activity necessary? Is there enough information to support the allegations that it can be carried on without undue harm to the environment? Are there better alternatives, or is there a reason to delay until we know more or have done better experimental work?

The reason we have not moved in this direction thus far is that we have not treated environmental resources as property entitled to be maintained and protected for the benefit of its owners, the public, subject to infringement only when it can be demonstrated that some other need is paramount and is being carried on with the minimum possible harm. Rather, we have treated those resources as the domain of no one, as wild fruits to be plucked at will by the first hungry claimant. We have designated a zero price for them, and we are reaping the inevitable consequence in the form of extravagant and largely unrestrained use.

What will happen if we begin to treat these resources as rights which citizens are entitled to maintain at law? Does this mean that no development can ever go forward, that we will be condemned to remain at a standstill without another tree cut, another stream dammed, or another road built? Of course the answer is a resounding no. Just as a landowner or first homebuilder in a neighborhood may not enjoin all subsequent homebuilding just because it would impair his unrestricted view of the scenery out of his living-room window, the public, as a holder of rights, has no absolute claim against developments which will affect that right. The public right to public resources, like private rights, must be subject to the reasonable demands of other users, whether they be factories, power companies, or residential developers.

Thus a public right to clean air will not necessarily be a right to maintain the air as fresh as it is on the top of the highest mountain. Rather, it will be a right to maintain it as clean as it ought to be to protect health and comfort when considered against the demands for spillover use of the air by other enterprises—and with due consideration of the need for such uses, the alternatives available to the enterprisers, existing and potential technology, and the possibility of other less harmful locations. Those are the issues at stake in environmental disputes to which courts must now begin to turn their attention.

Of course, no one can identify in advance the precise resolution of any given potential controversy. This is one of the reasons it is necessary to provide for the process of elucidating litigation, and this is why such litigation must go forward in the fashion of the common law—meeting individual cases on their particular merits, rather than in the restrictive style of conventional judicial review of administrative action.

It should be reiterated here that insofar as legislatures are satisfied that they know what balance ought to be struck in any given problem area—whether it be the proximity of airports to cities, the amount of mercury that can be dumped in a stream, or the availability of marshland for filling and development—they ought to embody those standards, with the greatest precision possible, in statutes, and thus minimize the need for common-law litigation. Until and unless that process covers the entire spectrum of environmental problems, however, there will remain a need for public action in the courtroom.

II

The preceding proposal for the establishment of public rights may seem astonishing to some readers, and it may seem doubtful that any such concept can be built into our legal system. For them, a brief backwards excursus into legal history is needed. The idea of public rights is, in fact, not new—it is as old as the ancient Roman law and the common law of England. Lamentably, it has been largely forgotten, and it is now time to revive and rejuvenate it, for in principle it is as vital as the environmental dilemmas we moderns find all around us.

Long ago there developed in the law of the Roman Empire a legal theory known as the "doctrine of the public trust." It was founded upon the very sensible idea that certain common properties, such as rivers, the seashore, and the air, were held by government in trusteeship for the free and unimpeded use of the general public. Our contemporary concerns about "the environment" bear a very close conceptual relationship to this venerable legal doctrine.

Under the Roman law, perpetual use of common properties "was dedicated to the public." As one scholar, R. W. Lee, noted: "In general the shore was not owned by individuals. One text suggests that it was the property of the Roman people. More often it is regarded as owned by no one, the public having undefined rights of use and enjoyment." Similarly in England, according to R. G. Hall, the law developed that "the ownership of the shore, as between the public and the King, has been settled in favor of the King: but . . . this ownership is, and had been immemorially, liable to certain general rights of egress and regress, for fishing, trading, and other uses claimed and used by his subjects."

American law adopted the general idea of trusteeship but rarely applied it to any but a few sorts of public properties such as shorelands and parks. The content and purpose of the doctrine never received a careful explication, though occasionally a comment can be found in the cases to the effect that it is "inconceivable" that any person would claim a private-property interest in the navigable waters of the United States, assertable against the free and general use of the public at large. And from time to time provisions can be found, as in the Northwest Ordinance of 1787, which stated that "the navigable waters leading into the Mississippi . . . shall be common highways and forever free . . . to the citizens of the United States. . . ."

The scattered evidence, taken together, suggests that the idea of a public trusteeship rests upon three related principles. First, that certain interests—like the air and the sea—have such importance to the citizenry as a whole that it would be unwise to make them the subject of private ownership. Second, that they partake so much of the bounty of nature, rather than of individual enterprise, that they should be made freely available to the entire citizenry without regard to economic status. And, finally, that it is a principle purpose of government to promote the interests of the general public rather than to redistribute public goods from broad public uses to restricted private benefit.

The indices of a trust problem do not lie merely in the fact that public property is being reallocated to a different use or even that some element of subsidy is involved, but rather in the absence of substantial evidence that some compensating public benefit is being achieved thereby. It is this latter fact that operates as a signal to the court that the public interest is under threat.

Subsidies to particular elements of the society are, of course, common and their legality unquestioned when the public benefit sought to be obtained is observable. Thus the provision of decent housing for the poor, the revitalization of a declining local economy or a fragile industry, to say nothing of free school lunches or public libraries, go unquestioned by the courts. But a judge can hardly avoid curiosity about the benefit sought to be achieved when valuable shoreland is conveyed to private purveyors of luxury housing at a fraction of its market value or where public fisheries are destroyed by an industrial dumping ground.

Courts have been alert to these problems, though the case law is not abundant. Not many years ago, a group of local citizens in Massachusetts challenged the attempt of an administrative agency—in this instance, a Tramway Authority—to convert a parkland reservation on Mount Greylock into a ski area.[1] Ordinarily, there would be no basis for doubting the propriety of a decision to convert public land from a low- to a high-intensity sort of recreational facility.

There was a peculiar feature of the plan which captured the court's attention, however. Existing ski facilities were apparently abundant enough in the area for the agency to find difficulty in arranging financing. As a result, it was compelled to comply with the demand of an investment banking firm that the agency turn the area over to a private professional resort firm under quite unattractive terms that required, among other things, a large share of the net income and extensive control over management.

As the court conceived the problem, it was not simply whether the agency had acted arbitrarily or without any possible authority in the statutes governing it; rather, there was a problem of the conformity of this proposal with any reasonable policy for the benefit of the public:

> The profit sharing feature and some aspects of the project strongly suggest a commercial enterprise. . . . we find no express grant to the Authority of power to permit use of public lands and of the Authority's borrowed funds for what seems, in part at least, a commercial venture for profit.

[1] Gould v. Greylock Reservation Commission, 350 Mass. 410, 215 N.E.2d 114 (1966).

The court concluded that such a venture should not be permitted to go forward. In essence, it enforced the public trust at the behest of private citizens objecting to the project.

The trust doctrine, as it developed in American law, has never held to the rigorous view that common property resources must be held in reserve from all private development or always be maintained in their traditional purity. Instead, a balance has been struck which is designed to retain the largest measure of public use consistent with needful development and industrialization. This standard, implemented in the intuitive manner characteristic of the common law, is more easily described than defined.

For example, some years ago, the City of Milwaukee granted shoreline land along Lake Michigan to a steel company in exchange for a tract the company held that was needed for building the harbor of Milwaukee. Objections were raised that public trust properties could never be so divested in favor of private interests. But the Wisconsin court quickly put this extreme argument into perspective. Harbors are perfectly appropriate public facilities with great potential public benefit; the exchange made by the City was reasonable and businesslike; and the adverse impact on traditional public recreational uses was trivial in comparison to the benefits to be derived and the remaining opportunities available along the shoreline of a vast inland sea. The court held:[2]

It is not the law . . . that the state, represented by its legislature, must forever be quiescent in the administration of the trust doctrine, to the extent of leaving the shores of Lake Michigan in all instances as in the same

[2] Milwaukee v. State, 193 Wis. 423, 214 N.W. 820 (1927).

condition and contour as they existed prior to the advent of the white civilization in the territorial area of Wisconsin. . . . The trust reposed in the state is . . . governmental, active and administrative. . . . The condition confronting the legislature was not a theory but a fact. This condition required positive action, and the legislature wisely and well discharged its duties. . . .

In succeeding cases, the Wisconsin court had to face a number of proposals for reallocating shore and parkland use, ranging from the enlargement of parking facilities at a recreation center to the construction of a public auditorium on fill at the shoreline of an inland lake. Drawing on principles set down in the Milwaukee case, it devised a set of guidelines for testing the reasonableness of a trust land use proposal that is as definitive as any judicial test yet devised.[3] Notably, the test incorporates in substantial degree each of the three basic values suggested earlier in this section. To be in conformity with the trust obligation, as applied to that case, the court said, the project should be such that

1. Public bodies will control the use of the area.
2. The area will be devoted to public purposes and open to the public.
3. The diminution of the lake will be very small when compared with the whole of [the lake].
4. No one of the public uses of the lake as a lake will be destroyed or greatly impaired.
5. The disappointment of those members of the public

[3] State v. Public Service Comm'n, 275 Wis. 112, 81 N.W.2d 71 (1957); Madison v. State, 1 Wis.2d. 252 N.W.2d 674 (1957).

who desire to boat, fish or swim in the area to be filled is negligible when compared with the greater convenience to be afforded those members of the public who use the city park.

Such a test, the cases make clear, is not meant to serve as a rigorous formula, but as a benchmark for unjustified diminution or degradation of public uses of common resources. As one examines the cases in other states where trust problems have received attention,[4] one sees the same themes recur—concern for public access, control by public agencies, respect for the maintenance of general use by the citizenry, and observable public benefits in exchange for any notable diminution of public uses.

The conflict between public use and private profit has an analogue in the wholly public sphere, where the problems of localism lead to concerns for excessively narrow benefits. Thus, around San Francisco Bay, each local community has an incentive to engage in fill projects that may return immediate local benefits, but that cumulatively diminish the opportunities for use of the bay by the whole constituency of citizens to whom the bay had been an accessible resource. In such cases, the job of the courts is to cast doubt upon the appropriateness of decision-making by entities representing a constituency narrower than the whole public that has an interest in the bay.[5] The goal is to encourage consideration and adoption of a bay-wide regulatory scheme, and that goal was significantly realized

[4] See Joseph L. Sax: "The Public Trust Doctrine in Natural Resource Law," 68 MICHIGAN LAW REVIEW at 471, (Jan. 1970).

[5] People *ex rel* San Francisco Bay C. & D.C. v. Town of Emeryville, 69 Cal.2d 544, 72 Cal. Rptr. 790, 446 P.2d 790 (1968); Save San Francisco Bay Ass'n v. City of Albany, No. 383, 480, Superior Ct., Calif., Alameda County.

by legislation enacted in California in 1969.[6] Similar developments occurred in Wisconsin where judicial attacks upon local boating regulation for lakes in which the entire state citizenry had a stake helped to promote legislative efforts to enact state-wide boating regulations.[7]

Even where a court's doubts are great enough to bring its injunctive powers into play, it is extremely rare for any court to find a project expressly authorized by the legislature so inherently bereft of public benefit that it could be held illegal. In general, the judicial role is exhausted by forcing legislative attention upon a dubious project and encouraging legislative responses to the broader problems and policies which such projects raise.

In an extremely rare case, a court *will* find conduct so utterly without possible public justification that it will hold it illegal without regard to the clarity of legislative authorization. Plainly, this is a judicial power which ought to be exercised with the greatest possible restraint, for its frequent use would undermine the very purpose for which courts ought principally to involve themselves in such cases —that is, to promote the democratic process.

The limited power to invalidate clear legislative authority was exercised many years ago in an extreme case, Illinois Central Railroad v. Illinois.[8] In 1869 the Illinois legislature

6 Ch. 713, (1969) Calif. Stats. 552 (Deering Supp. Aug. 1969).

7 Madison v. Tolzman, 7 Wis.2d 570, 97 N.W.2d 513 (1959). Richard W. Cutler: "Chaos or Uniformity in Boating Regulations? The State as Trustee of Navigable Waters," 1965. WISCONSIN LAW REVIEW at 311.

8 146 U.S. 387 (1892). It took the case many years to wend its way to the Supreme Court for final resolution. Though the legislature had changed its mind in the interim, the question before the court was the validity of a legislative grant duly made which the Railroad claimed created a non-revocable property right. See A. Dunham: *Preservation of Open Space Areas*, Appendix B, Welfare Council of Metropolitan Chicago, 1966.

conveyed to the railroad fee-simple title to more than a thousand acres of the most valuable land in the United States—the shore of Lake Michigan for a mile out from the coast and for a mile in length along the entire central business district of Chicago, from Randolph Street on the north to Twelfth Street on the south. Not only was the land of almost incalculable value even a century ago, but it comprised virtually the whole waterfront of the city available for water-borne commerce.

Even for those free-wheeling days of railroad politicking, this was a notable achievement for Illinois Central—so much so that four years later the legislature itself repented and repealed the grant. But the railroad said that a legislative grant of property, duly consummated, could not be undone: it was now the owner of the Chicago waterfront. This was too much for the Supreme Court—a legislature simply could not give away Lake Michigan and with it the essential powers of regulation over commerce. So much at least of the trusteeship responsibility is inherently an inalienable obligation of government and will be enforced even in the face of clear legislation.

Similarly, the Wisconsin legislature once gave a property owner authority to drain an entire lake of substantial size and convert it into a private plot—the court stopped that one too, despite laments that it was substituting its judgment for that of the duly elected lawmakers.[9] California courts also stepped in from time to time[1] to correct the abuses that finally came to light in the state's 1879 con-

[9] Priewe v. Wisconsin State Land and Imp. Co., 93 Wis. 534, 67 N.W. 918 (1896).

[1] E.g., Kimball v. MacPherson, 46 Cal. 104 (1873); Taylor v. Underhill, 40 Cal. 471 (1871); Ward v. Mulford, 32 Cal. 365 (1867).

stitutional convention, where the following was noted, among other things:

> The Central Pacific Railroad had bought up all the frontage on [San Francisco Bay], so that no other company could erect a wharf without its consent. . . . unscrupulous speculators had purchased tide lots and then tried to force owners of the abutting land to pay extortionate prices for mud flats, in order to attain access to the bay. . . . Swamp lands, tidelands and marsh and overflowed land had been taken in such vast quantities that now the people are hedged off entirely from reaching tide water, navigable water or salt water. . . . County surveyors unblushingly certified as lands "above low tide" thousands of acres that lay six to eighteen feet below the waters of San Francisco Bay. . . . But these patents were no more astonishing than others under which cattle barons and speculators acquired vast tracts of dry land in the Sacramento and San Joaquin Valley as "swamp land."[2]

While the trust doctrine has thus far been applied to a rather limited number of problems, plainly its underlying concept is readily adaptable to the whole range of issues that comprise our environmental dilemma—air and water pollution, the dissemination of pesticides, radioactivity, congestion, noise, and the destruction of natural areas and open space. Essentially, each problem is characterized by the spillover effects that developmental activity has upon common resources whose amenities (or adversities) are widely diffused over the general population; and by the

[2] M. Scott: *The Future of San Francisco Bay,* Institute of Governmental Studies, University of California, Berkeley, 1963.

difficulty with which ordinary market transactions reflect gains or losses to those common resources.

The courts have operated in public trust cases to provide a counterbalance to market forces. They treat common property resources as an asset belonging equally to each citizen, and they hold that this asset may be impaired only with the courts' very reluctant consent and then only when some clear compensating benefit can be provided for the beneficiaries of the trust.

Common property resources such as clean air and water need no longer be perceived as receptacles for the waste of industry or as free delicacies to be consumed at will by those hungry for profit, but rather as interests held in common by the entire citizenry. Like any private interest, these interests are entitled to legal protection, and their owners are entitled to the right of enforcement. The ancient legal maxim cited before, *sic utere tuo ut alienum non laedas* (use your own property in such a manner as not to injure that of another), can now be applied not only to disputes between owners, but also to disputes between factory owners, for example, and the public right to clear air; between the real estate developer and the public right to the maintenance of productive areas for fisheries and wildlife; or between the mining company that strips the earth and the public's interest in the preservation of natural amenities.

The implementation of trust doctrine as a public right will raise the questions toward which environmental litigation has been pointing with only limited success so far. What public need supports the project sought to be built, and does that need outweigh the losses to the public resource values it threatens? What alternatives to the project are available that will minimize or avoid infringement of the public "property" rights that might be adversely affected? What, if any, specific benefits to the public are being provided to compensate for the losses that the proposed activity will engender?

Only when we are ready to ask such questions and to recognize the legitimacy of public rights as equivalent to traditional private property interests will we truly be on the way toward creating an effective body of environmental law.

Chapter 8

Making Democracy Work: Remands to the Legislature

I

Because the public trust theory has slipped into the background of judicial thought, it is not easy to illustrate its contemporary use with a large sample of cases. There is, however, a modicum of modern cases in which courts, albeit indirectly, have employed the underlying concepts and techniques of public trust theory to indicate sufficiently the contemporary viability and effectiveness of this approach as a tool for dealing with environmental disputes.

The chapters which follow illustrate what *can* be done by sensitive and willing courts. The cases discussed in this particular chapter make use of the technique of the legislative remand—the device by which courts, at the behest of citizens suing in their capacity as members of the public, halt a project found to infringe public rights to some common resource. In so doing, the courts thrust upon the promoter of that project the affirmative obligation to go back to the legislature and obtain specific authorization (if he can get it) that makes clear a decisive public policy to subordinate traditional public use to some private or government use.

These cases are revealing in several respects. They show how judicial intervention is used to give the advocates of public uses a source of power (in the sense of shifting the legislative burden of proof) to make the public trust an enforceable reality. Moreover, they show the court operating to protect public rights without infringing the ultimate right of the legislative branch of government to make public policy decisions. And, finally, a consideration of the outcome of the cases shows how litigation can help promote a more open and forthright legislative consideration of disputes over public resource policy than they would routinely get.

In Massachusetts a series of illuminating cases arose in the context of the routine conflict between highways and parks. Parks are always a target for highway departments seeking land. Beyond the economic and engineering advantages of using undeveloped land, there is the convenient fact that trees do not talk back. In ordinary circumstances a highway department simply condemns or appropriates parklands under a very broad statutory power to acquire such lands as it deems necessary for its work. Massachusetts highway officials operated under a general law of this sort.

But the Massachusetts legislature had also made clear in many laws that it attached considerable importance to the development and maintenance of parks within the Commonwealth. As is so often the case, however, no detailed arrangement had been made for resolving conflicts between park and highway department use, nor had it been decided in whose hands the power of decision lay —that is, who or what would be the ideal entity to adjudicate such conflicts.

Making Democracy Work: Remands to the Legislature

In 1965 the Massachusetts Department of Public Works decided to fill a public lake known as Spy Pond as part of a plan to relocate a state highway. Public lakes, known as "Great Ponds" in Massachusetts, have a venerable and important place in that state's resource history—they were set aside as public facilities more than three hundred years ago and are subject to considerable legal protection, though no law specifically bars a highway department from exercising its power of eminent domain against them.

Concerned over the threat to Spy Pond, residents of the Town of Arlington sued to enjoin the fill proposal.[1] As is customary in such cases, they sought to bring their claim within the bounds of some traditional doctrine. Happily, they selected the rule that lands devoted to one public use could not be diverted to another inconsistent use without explicit legislative authorization.

While the rule had been devised to avoid unseemly conflicts between competing public agencies, which might continually condemn desired land back and forth, the plaintiffs in the Spy Pond case asked the court to apply this old rule to a situation in which private citizens were one of the contending parties. If they could get the court to agree, they would in essence have judicial recognition of the public trust concept—citizens would be able to argue the merits of maintaining public resources as against those of a proposed development. Moreover, such a ruling would circumvent the usual problem ordinary citizens face when they try to challenge administrative agency decisions—judicial deference to supposed agency

---

[1] Sacco v. Department of Public Works, 352 Mass. 670, 227 N.E.2d 478 (1967).

expertise—and it would require the matter to be sent back to the legislature for resolution.

By thus dressing their novel claim in traditional form, the plaintiffs succeeded in getting the court to adopt their position. The court made clear that it understood the significance of the case. Though the defendant agency asserted that it had been given sweeping power by the legislature, the court responded that the legislature had also expressed many times its concern for the maintenance of parklands.

The diversity of legislative concerns presented serious and important public policy issues, the court indicated; those issues could not be ignored simply because the highway agency had broad condemnation power as part of its general statutory authority.

The department's claim that it was merely "improving the lands of the Commonwealth" was met by a sharp judicial response: "[It] seems rather that the improvement of public lands which the legislature provided for . . . is to preserve such lands so that they may be enjoyed by the people for recreational purposes." The court held that the highway agency could not proceed unless it obtained specific legislative authority.

Despite the strong and explicit language of the decision, the Department of Public Works continued marching to its own tune. A year later it was back in court, this time to acquire some wetlands for its highway program. Again, suit was instituted by private citizens, in Robbins v. Department of Public Works.[2] The land in contention was Fowl Meadows, "wetlands of considerable natural beauty

---

[2] 355 Mass. 328, 244 N.E.2d 577 (1969).

. . . often used for nature study and recreation." The meadows were owned and administered by the Metropolitan District Commission, a state parkland agency, which had agreed with the Department of Public Works to transfer the meadows to it for highway use. The case is of particular significance because the defendant was not only the highway agency, but also the agency whose specific function it was to protect parklands for the public. Moreover, the statute under which the transfer was to be made required and had received approval by both the Governor and the State Council.

Suit was brought to enjoin the proposed transfer, and the court's willingness to entertain a citizens' suit against the combined public-interest determinations of all these guardians of the citizenry is a measure of the degree to which skepticism about administrative discretion in dealings with public resources had come in the Supreme Judicial Court of Massachusetts.

The statute under which this transfer was made was considerably more explicit in the powers it gave the highway department than that involved in the Spy Pond case. Even with these differences, the court held, the statute failed to "state with the requisite degree of explicitness a legislative intention to effect the diversion of use which the DPW seeks to accomplish." It then set out the standard it required as adequate evidence of legislative intent, a standard patently designed to thrust such matters explicitly upon public attention and to require the legislature to put specifically upon the record the reallocative policy it was undertaking. A court could hardly have made clearer its concern that the administrative process reflected inequalities in the balance of political power:

We think it is essential to the expression of plain and explicit authority to divert parklands, Great Ponds, reservations and kindred areas to new and inconsistent public uses that the legislature identify the land and that there appear in the legislation not only a statement of the new use but a statement or recital showing in some way legislative awareness of the existing public use. In short, the legislation should express not merely the public will for the new use but its willingness to surrender or forgo the existing use.

Finding the statute before it clearly inadequate by this test, the court ordered that the lands not be transferred to the Department of Public Works unless and until legislation authorizing such a transfer was duly enacted.

II

Ultimately, the usefulness of litigation like that just described must be tested by its impact on policy, rather than merely by its ingenuity in the use of legal doctrine. The question is whether courts do in fact serve to pry open the democratic process and provoke consequences that are responsive to the merits of the controversy and more reflective of the variety of public constituencies which have an interest in the dispute.

There can be no single answer to this question—the governmental process is too complex to produce uniform solutions and the scope of judicial intervention like that in the Massachusetts highway-park controversies too limited to provide wholly satisfactory data. Nonetheless, there is some highly interesting tentative information.

The Spy Pond case, for example, was taken back to the

Massachusetts legislature. The plaintiffs' lawyer reported that

> . . . the legislature enacted a bill granting the D.P.W. authority to take 4.7 acres of Spy Pond for the highway. The Department had wanted a much broader bill, but it was hoist by its own petard in that it had insisted throughout the litigation that all it needed was 4.7 acres.

The result, from the plaintiffs' perspective, was hardly a total victory. Yet it represented far more than the shaving of some acreage from the highway department's proposal. Most notably, the legislature refused to affirm the idea that it should accede in advance to the unquestioned judgment of the administrative agency. It undertook a reconsideration of the controversy and—significantly— utilized the information extracted in litigation as a basis for its judgment. The lawsuit forced the agency to do something it was not accustomed to doing—to reconsider its original plans and reduce them to the more limited demands it could support in the questioning atmosphere of a courtroom, where assertions would be examined and assumptions challenged. The agency's "discretion" was put to the test, and it yielded a substantially reduced claim on parkland.

When the Fowl Meadows case went back to the legislature, there were even more interesting developments. According to the attorney for the plaintiffs in that case,

> The legislature had more discussion over the Fowl Meadows than almost anything except the pay raise in 1969. . . . after a Herculean effort, the House of

Representatives in Massachusetts voted 134–90 to authorize a feasibility study of a westerly route such as we have been working for. However, our local Public Works Department brought out its troops, in the form of at least six men who spent most of the week in the State House and, after reconsideration, obtained a bill for an opposite route by the narrow score of 109–105. The Senate concurred after removing some amendments and the Governor has signed the bill. However, the whole subject of superhighway construction through the Metropolitan region has been put into the hands of a seven-man commission which is to report whether or not any new highways are needed. It seems to us that they will quite surely urge that this road be built (we have not objected to the need of such a road) but, in the meantime, the Governor has stated in public and written us that he will not permit the transfer of the requisite parkland.

What happened as a result of the Fowl Meadows case emphasizes both the catalytic nature of the judicial role and the diffuse, impressionistic nature of the governmental process. Judicial intervention in the Fowl Meadows and the Spy Pond cases did not result simply in a remand to the Massachusetts legislature for a particular decision; rather the willingness of the court in both cases to take jurisdiction served also to alert the legislature to the existence of a problem and to the presence of relatively widespread differences of public opinion. Among other things, the inadequacy of traditional one-dimensional agencies like the Department of Public Works was highlighted. The legislature was thus encouraged to reach out for other perspectives and a commission formed to concern itself with the broader issues involved. Whether or not such a commission can be highly successful, its presence operates to thrust public attention on the problem. A significant, but essentially moribund, issue is thus activated as a political matter.

Moreover, a close vote in the legislature on a hotly contested question is not likely to be ignored by elected public officials. The Massachusetts Department of Public Works has had to use up some political credits—it has pressed many legislators to take what will be viewed by a number of citizens as an antipark view. Legislators must now begin to ask themselves more directly than in the past where the balance really lies between public support for highways and for parks. And the Department of Public Works will no doubt get the message that it ought not to come asking for such sensitive votes of record unless it is prepared to back its demands with a persuasive case on its merits. As its demands must be made public, the opportunity rises for them to be debated publicly— objecting citizens, who previously had no forum, can now challenge highway agency proposals in the full light of public attention. They too, however, must now choose their controversies more carefully lest they dissipate the public support they have so arduously cultivated.

Finally, there is the Governor of Massachusetts. No longer can he quietly sign deeds or give approval in the silence of his office. His willingness to sign such deeds of public land and the demands for a public statement on his part, as in the Fowl Meadows issue, impose upon him the obligation to do some serious thinking about the posture he wishes to adopt as a trustee of the state's parkland resources.

The most decisive litigation success in Massachusetts came in the wake of the ski area case mentioned in the preceding chapter, *Gould v. Greylock Reservation Commission*. Though the doctrinal structure of the Mount Greylock case differed from those discussed above, like them it involved a victory by citizen plaintiffs against the proposed development of a commercial enterprise in a Massachusetts park. The story of the dispute is beautifully told by one of the principals, William Tague, in an article that appeared in the *Berkshire Review*.[3] His description cannot be improved upon:

> We had tried hard to kill the Authority in the Legislature in 1965, [prior to the successful court action] but failed. This was such an exhausting and frustrating experience that I hate to think about it. It was, as they say, a lesson in "political reality." The reality is that in the Massachusetts Legislature (in 1965, anyway) appeals to reason generally don't work; one must play the politicians at their own game, on their own terms, which means he who has the most votes wins. Votes are gotten by threats, maneuvering, and deals, or by arousing an outraged public and forcing the politicians to do right. We chose the latter route.
>
> We ran the gauntlet of committee hearings at the State House, some of which were postponed at the last minute, causing acute problems of communication with

[3] From William H. Tague: "The Rise and Evaporation of the Mount Greylock Tramway," *Berkshire Review*, Vol. III, no. 1 (Summer, 1967).

the people throughout the state who had planned to attend. We issued messages by mail and telegram to all 238 representatives and 40 senators on the many occasions that seemed crucial. . . . And we had a face-to-face meeting with Governor John A. Volpe in his State House office (Peabody had vacated the premises, victim of a primary defeat in 1964) . Volpe remained noncommittal.

We had filed two bills, one to abolish the Tramway Authority, and the other to prohibit commercial use of the reservation in the future. For some time they shuttled back and forth among various committees, whose recommendations, favorable or unfavorable, appeared to have little or no bearing on the way the full legislature voted. . . . Finally the bills were sidetracked into a "study" which, of course, was never made. . . .

It was a different story in 1966 [after the court decision]. Mostly because of our victory in the Supreme Court, but also greatly helped by the groundwork laid the year before, our new bills sailed through the committees, getting favorable reports everywhere. . . . We all believed the odds . . . were against us. However, the court decision had a greater impact that we had thought. We found that it was the turning point of the entire conflict. The tramway forces by this time were in disarray, if not shock. . . . The Pittsfield Association of Business and Commerce (ABC) . . . had been vigorous and damaging early in 1965, but a year later, for some strange reason, the ABC members voted overwhelmingly against the pro-tramway posture of the leadership, and that ended that. Some of our people had a hand in the reversal, naturally. After the court decision, we found we had the support of a majority of five or six of the nine-man Berkshire legislative delegation. And the voices from Adams [a town near Mount Greylock] slowly died away. So did the Tramway Authority, although not slowly. It vanished suddenly on September 5, 1966, Labor Day, when both branches of the legislature, by voice vote, passed the abolition bill.

The relative impact of a court's decision to intervene or not can never be precisely established, for we do not have the opportunity to impose laboratory controls on real situations. Occasionally, however, divergent approaches to similar problems in various states do provide intriguing comparisons. Analogous recent cases in Texas and Mississippi illustrate the point.[4] In both, citizens challenged state authorization to private companies to dredge in public waters for oyster shells. In both, the plaintiffs sought to cast doubt on the validity of the authorization because of some technical defect in the grant or some limitation in the authorizing statute. In both, the real concern, of course, was with the adverse impact of dredging upon the general ecology of the area, which served as feeding and breeding grounds for birds and aquatic life.

In the Texas case the challenge was dismissed on the triply technical grounds that the lawsuit was an unpermitted litigation against the state's sovereignty, that the order granting the permit was within the administrative agency's unreviewable discretion, and that the plaintiffs had no vested property rights at stake and thus no litigable

---

[4] Texas Oyster Growers Association v. Odom, 385 S.W.2d 899 (Tex. Ct. Civ. App. 1965), writ of error refused n.r.e.; Parks v. Simpson, 242 Miss. 894, 137 So.2d 136 (1962).

interest in the controversy (though the plaintiffs were principally commercial fishermen reliant on the fishery resources of the bay for their livelihood) .

In the Mississippi case, a taxpayer's suit against the Marine Conservation Commission—to void a contract it had made to dredge for oyster shells—succeeded, though each of the grounds for dismissal used in the Texas case might have been invoked. Passing over such concerns, the court looked at the commission's statutory authority to lease tidewater bottoms and construed it narrowly to find that oyster shells were a part of the public trust that the commission had not been expressly authorized to sell.

While these cases had some technical legal differences, they were not sufficient to bind the courts to one approach or the other. The Mississippi court would have been perfectly free, had it so desired, to sustain the commission's exercise of discretion in the absence of explicit violation of statute, fraud, or corruption. Similarly, the Texas court could have gone beyond the fact that shell dredging was in general legal, to ask whether the particular leases in question were consistent with the obligation of the state to protect public rights to the use and enjoyment of water resources—an approach often taken in such cases. Even the ability of fishermen to sue to enforce the public right of fishery—flatly denied by the Texas court—has been clearly recognized in a number of other states.

The Parks case in Mississippi used a narrow statutory interpretation to declare an effective moratorium on decisions that seemed to raise serious dangers for important public resources and to have been inadequately considered either by the legislature or the administrative agency. Subsequent to the Parks case, the Mississippi legislature enacted a law conditioning shell-dredging permits upon approval by a three-fifths vote of the entire membership of the State Marine Conservation Commission, which approval must include that of its marine biologist member; there must, moreover, be a finding that "the dredging will not be deleterious to the aquatic life and harmful to the fishing industry," which finding must be "spread full upon the minutes of the Commission." By contrast, the shell-dredging controversy in Texas has dragged on inconclusively since 1966 in both the state and federal legislatures and within both state administrative agencies and the U.S. Army Corps of Engineers.

Judicial intervention as a technique to thrust a problem of significance upon a busy legislature's attention does pay dividends. While the Mississippi and Massachusetts cases discussed above went through the entire judicial structure up to the state supreme courts, judicial intervention often has its greatest impact long before appellate decisions are issued—often, indeed, before a case ever goes to trial.

Early in 1969 it was reported that the New Jersey legislature had voted to put to referendum a proposal to confirm the titles of private landowners to hundreds of square miles of valuable marsh and meadowland, public ownership of which had recently been recognized in hard-fought litigation. The proposal was drafted in conventional involuted legal terminology, and the Governor felt that it failed clearly to explain the important issues which were at stake. The legislature refused to amend the language, and the Governor—in a most extraordinary move —filed suit charging that the proposed amendment, as worded, was a fraud upon the right of the voters to be clearly and effectively informed.[5] The suit obtained widespread publicity under headlines referring to the "giveaway referendum." The legislature backed down and took the item off the ballot before the case went to trial. Of course the Governor was a Democrat fighting a Republican-dominated legislature, but the point is still valid. Had the Governor not sued, concerned citizens might have done the job for him.

The very prospect of judicial inquiry is itself a powerful weapon. While lawsuits may not and should not be brought simply to obtain publicity, it is a fact of life that the filing of a suit is news. Citizens have found out time and again that while informal objections are routinely ignored by the press, the presentation of a complaint to a court clerk is generally considered newsworthy.

Because the ultimate object of environmental cases is to activate the democratic process—and not simply to obtain a legal precedent isolated from the real world—such publicity considerations must not be ignored. It cannot be emphasized too strongly that the governmental process *is* a process—diffuse, interlocking, interdependent—and that any discussion of what courts can do, or what legislatures should do, must never lose sight of the fact that it is how we are governed that is in issue, not some academic theory about the purity of institutions. Again Mr. Tague, on the Greylock tramway case, went directly to the heart of the matter:[6]

> I felt that tactics should be geared mainly to action, and secondarily to hard words—hammer blows where it

[5] Hughes v. Blair, No. C-1528-68, Superior Court N.J., Ch. Div.—Mercer Co. (filed Feb. 19, 1969).
[6] Tague, *op. cit.*

hurt, rather than the usual conservationist rhetoric. The court case would stick to the question of the legality of what the Authority and Reservation Commission had done. The legislative fight, I hoped, would be waged purely in a political way—twisting arms and getting votes—particularly in the eastern part of the state where most of the votes are. Conservation is good and Greylock is beautiful and all that, but if they didn't vote for us they might find themselves out of a job after the next election. As it turned out, naturally, I suppose, there were all sorts of blurrings and overlappings of these separations. In the court testimony and in statements made before legislative committees a large amount of material dealt with the rarity of the Bicknell's thrush, the therapeutic value of unspoiled wilderness, and the uniqueness in Massachusetts of Greylock's Canadian zone. This may have had some intangible effect, but in fact the final results were gained in the courts on strictly legal grounds, and at the State House by means of raw political power.

During my investigation of the Hunting Creek matter, a question put in every interview was what significance should be attached to the lawsuit filed by those objecting to the project. There was some feeling that it may have stopped the imminent initiation of construction or that it may have been a deterrent to the obtaining of needed title insurance, though almost everyone agreed that the ongoing congressional investigation was fully adequate to assure that bulldozers would not suddenly appear and begin work —the risks of flaunting the Congress were simply too great.

One local Virginia resident noted that while it was difficult to attribute any specific consequences to the suit, it seemed clear to him, as a close observer of the controversy, that the suit had great importance of quite a different kind. It served as a "benchmark of seriousness of intent on the part of those who opposed the project."

A good deal turned on the attitudes of local public officials, he noted, and it is always difficult for such officials to develop a sense of community feeling. Letter-writing campaigns, organizational resolutions, public statements, and the like are cheap and easy. While they are not irrelevant, such activities do not tend to discriminate very well between deeply felt issues and those as to which objections are essentially superficial. A lawsuit, however, has quite another flavor to it—perhaps that is what makes it seem particularly newsworthy. To undertake a lawsuit requires serious commitments. Plaintiffs must be found who will formally attest to matters of consequence; substantial sums of money must be raised; professionals must be hired and asked to invest their time and standing on the charges made; experts must often be recruited; and witnesses must be prepared to subject themselves to extended examination under oath. While the difficulty of organizing for such activity has the undesirable effect of deterring some action which ought to be taken immediately, it also gives a stamp of importance to those cases which are prosecuted diligently.

For these reasons, there is a tendency to take the institution of a lawsuit seriously, and for public officials the initiation and pursuit of such litigation is often a signal to reconsider their positions or to adopt positions formerly avoided. The point is an intriguing one, for it implies a role for the court that is fulfilled passively—simply by its availability and its status as an institution not to be trifled with—and that very usefully plays into the political process.

The cases described here illustrate one way in which courts can confront and deal with the claims of public right which underlie the public trust theory. Not only do they serve to give legal status to public claims, but by employing the technique of the legislative remand, they focus attention upon the limitations of the administrative agency and put environmental policy issues squarely before the legislature.

Chapter 9

A Pause
in Time:
The Moratorium

I

Sometimes the obligation of government to protect the public trust is explicitly recognized in statutory form. In such situations, the problem is not to achieve recognition of public rights, but to assure that some mechanism is made available for their implementation. The problem is a pervasive one, for legislatures find it easy to declare, in large terms, their concern for the protection of the public interest. The question is what happens between the statutory declaration and the ultimate disposition of the interests that are supposed to be protected by those declarations.

The answer, frequently, is that they are left to the determination of some relatively low-level administrator out in a regional agency office. This problem was clearly illustrated by a recent case challenging the management of the national forests by the U.S. Forest Service.

In 1964 Congress passed the Wilderness Act, setting aside certain federal lands still in pristine condition, safeguarding them from lumbering, structures, roads, and other evidences of man's work. Among its many provisions, the Wilderness Act imposed upon the Secretary of Agriculture, who has general charge of the national forest system, the obligation to complete within a period of ten years a review of forest lands suitable for addition to, or withdrawal from, the wilderness system.

The establishment of a wilderness system is, of course, nothing more than a particular application in statutory form of public trust theory. It asserts that the right of the general public to a permanent reservation of pristine land areas must take its place along with such other insistent demands upon forest resources as commercial timber-cutting.

Because Congress was not prepared in 1964 to identify for all time all the lands which should be reserved as wilderness, some mechanism had to be created for examining and resolving the inevitable conflicts that would occur between wilderness use and commercial timber-harvesting. The scheme adopted was that of the review mentioned above. Areas potentially suitable for wilderness inclusion were to be reviewed by the Secretary within a period of ten years, and recommendations were to be forwarded to the President and then to Congress. Congress reserved to itself the final determination, area by area, of modifications in the national wilderness system. For the guidance of administrative officials, the law set out a relatively detailed definition of "wilderness"[1] and thereby

[1] The act defines "wilderness" as follows: "An area of undeveloped Federal land retaining its primeval character and influence, without permanent improvements or human habitation . . . which generally appears to have been affected primarily by the forces of nature, with the imprint of man's work substantially unnoticeable; has outstanding opportunities for solitude or a primitive and unconfined type of recreaton; . . . is of sufficient size as to make practicable its preservation and use in an unimpaired condition; and may also contain ecological, geological, or other features of scientific, educational, scenic, or historical value." Act of Sept. 3, 1964, P.L. 88-577, § 2 (c), 78 Stat. 890, 16 U.S.C. § 1131 (c).

of those lands which were deserving of study with a view toward their inclusion in the wilderness system.

The mechanism thus devised seems a sensible one for implementing the public trust, and it is—so long as administrators can be trusted implicitly to carry out the spirit and the letter of the law. But what if the Forest Service fails? If it decides that certain areas, even though they meet the statutory definitions, are not worthy of preservation as wilderness or even of submission to Congress for its judgment? If the Forest Service simply contracts with a lumber company for commercial harvesting of trees on a tract that citizens reasonably believe belong within the wilderness system? And what if the lumbering, under a Forest Service contract, is scheduled to go forward imminently?

Here is where the device of the judicial moratorium comes into play and where it becomes critical to distinguish between a public right that is simply declared in a statute and one that is enforceable in law at the behest of private citizens.

This was precisely the situation in the White River National Forest in Colorado, where the Forest Service had sold an area asserted to have wilderness qualities to a lumber company. Local citizens filed suit in the U.S. District Court to enjoin the sale,[2] claiming the right to a judicially declared moratorium until the matter could be brought to the attention of Congress so it could determine whether

[2] Parker v. United States, 309 F. Supp. 593 (D. Colo. 1970). The plaintiffs were residents and property owners in the area, a professional wilderness guide, the Sierra Club and the Eagles Nest wilderness Committee. The defendants were the Secretary of Agriculture, the Chief of the Forest Service, the Regional Forester, and the Supervisor of the White River National Forest.

the policy and purpose of the wilderness law were being violated by an administrative *fait accompli.*

Government lawyers responded in predictable fashion. No mere citizen could sue to enforce the Wilderness Act, they said. What Congress had created, they claimed, was not a right enforceable by members of the public, but a direction to the Forest Service to exercise *its* discretion, and if it exercised that discretion erroneously, the citizens could always bring their complaints to Congress. These lawyers failed to note, of course, that by the time citizens could get to Congress (which has a few other priority matters on its agenda) , the wilderness they sought to save would probably already have been cut over by the lumber company.

Thus, two of the central issues in environmental litigation were squarely put to the court. Is the legislative declaration of environmental standards a right, enforceable as a trust obligation by citizens claiming to be the beneficiaries of the trust and thereby the principal parties in interest? And is the court able and willing to act effectively in support of such a claim with a moratorium, instead of merely mouthing platitudes about taking one's problems to the legislature?

Government lawyers, those eminent guardians of the public interest, wheeled out all their heavy artillery in a concerted effort to persuade the court not to hear the case. Lawsuits of this kind, they gravely intoned, threaten the democratic process—"people may remove their elected representatives," they said, "as they cannot dismiss United States judges. . . . the plaintiffs face a political decision, i.e. to convince the Congress to pass an act. . . ." Moreover, they said—as if Congress had decreed the cutting of these trees and as if the courts mindlessly gave out injunctions to any passerby who asked for one,

> Projects planned by the executive branch and funded by the legislature . . . [would] be frustrated by the judicial branch at the whim of any citizen who disagrees with the justification of such projects.
>
> .   .   .
>
> If the plaintiffs have standing to have the court review the judgment of the foresters to cut or not to cut public timber, the next step would be review of employment practices, procurement procedure, the location of offices and finally what segment of the public is to be favored.

Assertions like this typify the indiscriminate way in which government lawyers tend to polarize the issues in such cases. In any given case, it may or may not be that procurement or employment practices raise important public policy questions. It hardly seems appropriate to assume that they will not, rather than leaving that question to be decided in a discrete context. It would undoubtedly be the rare case in which a plaintiff could satisfy a court that routine decisions about office locations for federal agencies raise significant public issues; if they do not, cases involving such questions can be, and are, promptly dismissed by the courts. One wonders why government briefs, devoted in such cases to assuring judges that administrative discretion should be trusted implicitly, are so ready to assume that judges themselves are such fools or such puppets that they cannot be trusted to make rational distinctions between substantial and frivolous claims.

If, for example, the case appeared to involve no more than a disputed judgment of technical expertise, then one might well agree with the government that "Congress ha[d] wisely left these technical matters to the technicians . . . in deciding whether merchantable trees are to be harvested or left to die." No judge is likely to stop an ongoing program to inquire into such matters. But that is not what the Parker case involved at all. The issue was much broader and involved far more important matters of national policy. The question was upon what basis the broad lines were to be drawn in allocating national forest lands among timber supply, developed recreation areas, and wilderness, and—more importantly—whether, and under what circumstances, that judgment is to be preempted from congressional purview.

Just how far removed the Parker case was from what the government called a "judgment in technical matters" was illustrated, ironically, by the government itself. In 1967 one of the plaintiff groups sent to the Secretary of Agriculture a proposal to include within the wilderness system the area subsequently sold for lumbering. They received in reply a long letter from an Assistant Secretary in the Agriculture Department noting the absence in their proposal of detailed quantification of needs, benefits, and costs. A proper analysis, he said, required an estimate of the relative needs for timber and wilderness, population growth, recreation demand, and a host of other factors.

A dozen Solomons could hardly begin to answer in detail all the questions he raised, though they were obviously relevant considerations. The point is that they went far beyond any "technical" decision about whether certain mature trees ought to be harvested. They were policy questions of considerable magnitude, and though essentially unanswerable in any rigorous fashion, they—like all live matters of public policy—had to be dealt with. The problem was whether they were ultimately to be left to the supervisor of the White River National Forest and his counterparts or to be reserved for the judgment of Congress.

It was at this point that the question of judicial intervention arose. Plainly the plaintiffs did not want the court to answer these questions—they only wanted it to determine that there were issues of consequence at stake regarding the challenged area and that it was reasonable to withhold an irreversible judgment on them pending review and recommendations—which had not yet been presented by the Secretary of Agriculture for ultimate transmission to Congress—and consideration of those recommendations by Congress.

Thus the question truly before the court was plain and nontechnical and surely not beyond the ken of a federal judge: why was the Forest Service so eager to sell off this controversial tract, asserted to have wilderness qualities, prior to the review of, and recommendations for, that area under the Wilderness Act? The question was natural enough, for the White River National Forest was full of harvestable timber, and there were already a number of nearby areas in which logging had gone forward and that no one wanted to include in the wilderness system.

As the lawsuit ultimately revealed, the decision to offer this tract for sale in 1969 was actually made seven years earlier—in 1962, before the Wilderness Act became law. At that time, the Forest Service produced a ten-year plan that designated the controversial area for fiscal year 1969 lumbering. The reasons, notably, were perfectly *non*arbitrary and *non*capricious—they were quite rational *from the perspective of an agency concerned with lumber production.* An access road had already been planned. The trees in this area were—in forest industry parlance—mature and overmature; they were ripe for cutting. And they were apparently subject to a bark-beetle problem that argued for cutting relatively soon. There is no evidence in the voluminous report prepared by the Forest Service that any considerations other than silvicultural ones affected their judgment. Subsequent studies and reports in 1966 and 1967 simply carried forward the judgment of the earlier ten-year plan, with no indication that ensuing events in Congress were of any moment—a disturbing revelation, but not a surprising one for it cannot be emphasized too strongly that the enactment of laws in Washington does not miraculously change the perspectives and practices of established administrative agencies.

This point was not lost on the judge, William E. Doyle, who quickly cut through the professional jargon of government witnesses and asked: "Where is the compelling public interest in selling the timber? That's what I'd like to know."

It did not take him long to conclude that there was no acceptable answer to this question. "The thrust of the testimony was that the presence of a road commits the area to industry use," he observed. "They [the government witnesses] assume the existing road would more or less go to waste if they didn't use it for industry purposes. That's their philosophy."

Having failed in their first strategy, the defendants regaled the judge with the prospect of mills closing, lost jobs, and a national shortage of timber. At this, Judge Doyle leaned forward and said:

> This parade of horribles doesn't impress me at all. I don't think the sky will fall, and I don't accept this "Chicken Little" approach to the law. One little judicial decision isn't going to disturb the mazes of bureaucracy described to me today—it won't even cause a ripple.

The explanation sought by Judge Doyle of the Forest Service's need to go forward with its cutting program in the challenged area was never forthcoming. Finding that there was no need for immediate action and that the area did have wilderness quality, he declared a moratorium on cutting unless and until Congress had an opportunity to express itself.

II

It is instructive to look beyond the details of Parker v. United States—which had the benefit of a statute explicitly approving case-by-case congressional review—to the larger implications of the judicially declared moratorium. For the question necessarily arises whether such relief in a case like this does not simply shift the burden of obtaining legislative action from one of the combatants to another. If the plaintiffs had gone to Congress and obtained a law enacting the disputed area into the wilderness system (which could lawfully have been done even before the Secretary of Agriculture reviewed the area), the controversy would have been resolved. Why not, then, leave that burden upon them and relieve the courts from the inevitable difficulties of a novel type of litigation?

In the abstract, it might seem a matter of indifference whether a court says (1) it would seem desirable to find out what the legislature thinks about this proposal, and therefore the plaintiffs should go to Congress and urge them to consider the matter; or (2) legislative action would seem desirable, and therefore the court is going to enjoin the government unless and until Congress resolved the controversy.

The choices seem a matter of difference, however, only if it is assumed that access to the legislature is itself wholly a matter of indifference and that there are no meaningful inequalities between the ability of a private citizens' group and that of a federal cabinet department to get an issue onto the congressional agenda. Here is another of the focal points where citizen-initiated litigation confronts a deep-seated and unexamined assumption about the governmental process. One need not be much of an expert to know that it is extremely difficult to get a legislature to act on a matter, one way or the other—even the President has his problems here. A case like Hunting Creek, at the state level, illuminates how unequal effective access to the legislature can be. Those interest groups and agencies with regular and continuous legislative business have associations that greatly facilitate their opportunities to be heard. But not always—sometimes even the most powerful and experienced interests cannot get the hearings they want, sometimes small and inexperienced groups have surprising successes, and sometimes luck or timing may be critical. The realities are variable, for the system itself is loose-jointed.

A judge can ignore the realities and presume that everyone who ought to be heard will be heard in time, on the assumption that in the legislative process, as in a bakery shop, one takes his number and waits his turn. Or, adjusting flexibly to the situation before him, he can focus attention on the desirability of trying to assure that an important matter *does* get heard in a timely fashion. Such a judge will issue no timeless, philosophical *bon mots*—instead he might respond to a case like Parker v. United States in the following fashion: If the plaintiffs are to be remitted to their own initiative in getting legislative action, they may or may not get a hearing before the timber is cut. If the cutting is anticipated in a few weeks or months, the chances of obtaining legislative consideration and resolution is remote. Once the cutting proceeds, the issue is resolved *ipso facto,* so unless there is some demonstrated need for cutting this area soon that is at least as important as the policy plaintiffs want to have resolved, less damage is incurred by enjoining cutting than in failing to do so.

Moreover, since the goal is to obtain congressional consideration, the court has a choice in deciding upon which group—plaintiffs or defendants—to impose the burden of obtaining legislative action. It would seem desirable to impose the burden upon the group most likely to be effective in prodding Congress. Surely it seems likely that a cabinet department of the federal government is better situated in this respect than a relatively obscure group of private citizens. If the matter is thought important enough, it can be sent up the Agriculture Department chain of command to the Secretary, who has regular and professional liaison with Congress. In every operative situation, the key to success is knowing where the critical people are and working through them. In this situation, the entity with the greatest leverage to obtain the desired goal—congressional consideration—is the Secretary of Agriculture.

A court's decision to put the onus upon the Secretary can fulfill another of the plaintiff's requests, and a reasonable one; it imposes pressure upon the government at a significant policy level to decide whether the issue is important enough to deserve priority status on its legislative agenda. If the Secretary does not feel it is important enough, or if upon further consideration he does not feel prepared to fight against wilderness designation, then no great harm is likely to be done in letting the plaintiffs prevail by governmental inaction. In any event, Agriculture Department inaction merely defers the question of wilderness designation versus timbering; permitting the timbering forecloses it.

While an argument can be made that the plaintiff's ability to mobilize political forces to get Congress to act is also a measure of the importance they attach to the question, it is undoubtedly going to take more time, effort, and money to organize an exceedingly diffuse and relatively inexperienced constituency than it would to mobilize the legislative resources of the Department of Agriculture. Since no one benefits by delaying legislative action (which is the ultimate goal), it is appropriate to impose the burden upon that entity which is best equipped to carry it.

In the particular setting of the Parker case, the problem was not as open-ended as it might have been. Since the plaintiff's claim was tied to the ultimate status of a nearby primitive area—a status which, under the law, would soon have to be suggested to Congress with some recommendation—it would seem appropriate to enjoin cutting only until Congress receives *and disposes* of the recommendations dealing with the area. One consequence of this approach might be to expedite review of that particular area, a job that should in any event have been completed before timber-cutting decisions were made final.

Notably, such an order enjoining cutting would not prevent earlier action. If the Secretary of Agriculture felt strongly enough, he might well prevail on Congress to legislate for the noninclusion of the area in the wilderness system. If he could achieve that result quite quickly, he would be able to go forward with his own programs soon. Or Congress itself might act quickly one way or the other. It could be anticipated that the flexibility of such an arrangement, with the principal burden borne, or immediate action taken by, a well-situated agency such as a cabinet department, would mitigate most problems of unwarranted delay. Certainly if the Secretary or a private party believed there were an urgency about the matter which could not be accommodated within the time needed to obtain legislative action, they should be allowed to argue that issue before the court. It is customary for judges to have to weigh competing demands of imminent and irreversible harm in cases where injunctive relief is sought, and it should not be assumed that they will be less able to cope with claims of exigency here than in the generality of matters which come before them.

III

The judicially declared moratorium is an innovation to which tradition-bound lawyers will not find it easy to accommodate themselves, yet few problems in the burgeoning area of environmental law so fittingly demonstrate the inadequacies of our conventional and excessive attachment

to the idea of separation of powers among the branches
of government. Obviously, the separation principle is both
needful and appropriate up to a point—we cannot, for
example, have judges appropriating monies for the salaries
of government employees nor permit legislatures to enforce
common-law contractual rights. The moratorium, however, does illustrate the appropriateness of judicial intervention at times to act in aid of rational decision-making
by the other branches of government.

Where, as in the Colorado wilderness case, injunctive
relief is sought to enjoin private use of public lands, no
dramatic departures from traditional legal principles are
required. Occasionally, however, the moratorium will
have to be sought to prevent private use of privately owned
land pending legislative action, and in such instances,
ordinary notions about the scope of private property rights
are put to rather a severe test.

This very problem was presented in another Colorado
case in 1969, in what is undoubtedly one of the most extraordinary lawsuits yet to arise in the area of environmental
litigation. Some thirty-five miles west of Colorado Springs
is a large tract of privately-owned land known as the
Florissant Fossil Beds; there, embedded in thin layers of
shale thirty-four million years ago, rest examples of plant
and fish remains that are conceded by scientists to be
among the finest and richest specimens of their kind anywhere in the world. They are, according to a distinguished
expert from the U.S. Geological Survey, "to geology, pale-
ontology and evolution, what the Rosetta Stone was to
Egyptology and the Dead Sea Scrolls [were] to Christi-
anity."

For a number of years a proposal had been before Congress to acquire the tract and create a Florissant Fossil Beds National Monument. As with so many such bills, this one had dragged its langorous way indecisively through the legislature. By June 1969 the proposal had finally passed the Senate and was pending before a committee of the House of Representatives. Then a group of real estate developers purchased the tract for $150 an acre and moved with extraordinary speed to begin development. On July 2 it was learned that the developers were planning within a matter of days to begin bulldozing a road through the proposed national monument on their privately owned land. Citizen requests for delay, pending congressional action, were ignored, though it was reported that the owners were willing to sell their land—acquired only five weeks earlier—for $350 an acre; eighteen-hundred acres of the intended development lay within the proposed national monument.

On July 3 an *ad hoc* citizen group, calling itself Defenders of Florissant, filed suit in the U.S. District Court in Denver seeking an injunction until Congress completed action on the pending bill.[3] The case came before Judge Hatfield Chilson on a motion for immediate temporary injunction relief. Chilson denied the motion, ruling that no legal standard permitted him to restrain this private use of private land.

Chilson ruled against the plaintiffs on July 9; the next day an emergency motion was put before the U.S. Court of Appeals (Tenth Circuit) and was argued and decided that day (take note, commentators on the cumbersomeness and delay of the judicial process!).

[3] Defenders of Florissant, Inc. v. Park Land Co., No. C-1539, U.S. Dist. Ct., Colo.

The appeal was argued before a three-judge panel headed by Judge Jean S. Breitenstein. "But what statute does this excavation violate?" Judge Breitenstein asked. "Your honor," the plaintiffs' lawyer, Victor Yannacone, replied, "there is no direct statutory protection for fossils." Breitenstein continued: "What right have we to control the use of private land unless there's a nuisance perpetrated by the owners?" Yannacone answered: "Your honor, if someone had found the original U.S. Constitution buried on his land, and wanted to use it to mop up a stain on the floor, is there any doubt in the mind of this court that they could be prevented?"

That day the court granted a restraining order. The case was returned to Judge Chilson in the District Court, who again refused to grant an injunction, and again the plaintiffs returned to the Court of Appeals. It renewed the injunction on July 30, the day before the bill was scheduled to be acted upon in Congress. In handing the judges' order to the plaintiffs' lawyer, the clerk of the Court of Appeals said: "Will you please get that bill through Congress soon, and give us some rest."

On August 20, 1969, Public Law 91-60, establishing the Florissant Fossil Beds as a protected national monument, became law.

IV

The White River and Florissant fossil bed cases demonstrate the use of the judicial moratorium to protect legislative jurisdiction from both public and private shortsightedness. Each of these cases, though highly novel in its own way, dealt with a matter that was in a sense pending before the legislature. Thus, the judicial action taken in each case could be explained as merely designed to protect the right of Congress to act on a matter in which it had already indicated its desire to express its views. In this respect, neither case is as radical a departure from tradition at it might seem; nor does either imply that courts generally are as yet attuned to the underlying need for a moratorium to promote, as well as to protect, needed reexamination of doubtful administrative action.[4]

The judicially declared moratorium may have to be used in a less conventional setting, where the plaintiff is unable to rest his claim upon some pending legislative jurisdiction. From time to time, for example, controversies arise over programs which were authorized with no particular concern about environmental consequences, possibly because at the time they were initiated there was not enough information or concern about environmental effects to raise doubts or because the program was begun in (possibly justifiable) secrecy. Projects involving atomic energy or chemical and biological warfare exemplify the problem. On a more mundane level, the issue is illustrated by a case filed against a Corps of Engineers canal-building

---

[4] For example, in another recent case against the Forest Service, plaintiffs could not assert, as they did in Parker v. United States that the area in question was one which Congress had expressly desired to review under the Wilderness Act. They could only claim that under the general law for national forest management the Forest Service had employed an excessive imbalance in favor of timber-harvesting. The judge threw them out of court, noting that under the existing legal structure, the plaintiffs "can only prevail if they can establish by clear and convincing proof that the action of the defendants is arbitrary and capricious and not in accordance with law. . . . It must appear that the action of the agency was in effect malicious and illegal. . . ." Gandt v. Hardin, Civ. Action No. 1334, U.S. Dist. Ct. W. Dist., Mich., N. Div. (opinion of Judge W. Wallace Kent, Dec. 11, 1969).

program, first authorized in 1942 in the interest of national defense, that has continued on into the 1970's without being given a fresh legislative review in light of newly found concern for the environment.[5]

Grave concern may arise later in the scientific community itself about the environmental aspects of such programs, and efforts to persuade the administrators to reconsider them may be unavailing. Similarly, the state of scientific knowledge may be such that no one can speak with certainty about long-term consequences—there may be nothing more than good reason to think adverse consequences may occur and that if they occur, they may be very serious. There may, for example, be reason to fear the accumulation of toxic substances within a population, important changes in the climate, or notable modification in oceanic resources. In short, there may be evidence enough to persuade a reasonable man that a moratorium is in order, considering the risk of harm and (if the facts support the conclusion) that no equally grave consequences are to be apprehended from withholding or withdrawing action.

A number of contemporary environmental problems seem to be of this kind. There is a great deal which we do not know and which a reasonably prudent man would want to know before he acts. Evidence might show that the balance between the risk of harm, though uncertain, and the benefits to be derived from immediate action favor delay. Yet a program might be continuing, or might have been authorized, in the absence of full knowledge or under cir-

5 Environmental Defense Fund v. Corps of Engineers, Civil Action No. 2655-69, U. S. Dist. Ct., D.C. (2d amended complaint, filed Apr. 9, 1970).

cumstances where the facts seem to have been buried under political exigency.

In such circumstances, the interposition of a judicially declared moratorium may be needed. It can be used either to liberate a legislature from an unwise program it finds it difficult to squelch or to provide the incentive for a needed sober second look. Such cases have not yet been developed. For the reasons indicated earlier in this book, it is hard to obtain judicial action unless the plaintiff is prepared to point to some specific statutory provision which has been violated. The adoption of the public trust theory and the development of a common-law approach to environmental cases, emphasizing the right to reasonable protection of common resources against serious threats of infringement in the absence of compensating benefits, can set the stage for cases of the kind just described. Too often we act in ignorance; an enforceable public right to delay action when more knowledge is needed is central to the development of the emerging law of environmental rights. As the concept of the public trust develops, the judicial moratorium will be available to meet this need.

Chapter 10

Litigating Environmental Issues

Thus far consideration has been given to those cases in which the courts operated to activate the legislative process or promote scientific work so that policy conflicts could be resolved or needed polices could be formulated in a timely fashion. Even in such cases, where court orders are designed only as a holding action until legislative resolution can be obtained, judges must satisfy themselves that the environmental threat is sufficient to warrant intervention. Thus courts must concern themselves with the merits of the controversy, and this raises the question of judicial competence to deal with what are usually considered technical and scientific matters.

The cases discussed in the preceding chapters should already have indicated that the usual fears about judicial competence are largely unwarranted, for it is not ordinarily an administrator's technical judgment that is called into question, but his judgment about policy matters. This was clearly indicated in the Colorado wilderness case, as it was in the Massachusetts highway-parkland cases and the Mount Greylock case where a commercial ski area was to displace a less-developed public recreation area.

Nevertheless, the preceding discussion has not detailed the

ways in which a court brings its skills to bear specifically upon claims of unreasonable threats to the environment. Nor have the cases thus far indicated the opportunities for final judicial resolution of controversies that need no further legislative consideration. Obviously, there are a good many situations of this kind—where the public policy is relatively clear and where the need is for direct enforcement rather than for a reopening of the legislative process. Of course, even in such cases the legislature remains free to change its policy or to correct a court decision that it considers misguided.

As the public trust concept begins to be more fully developed in the common law, cases appropriate for definitive judicial resolution will inevitably increase. Today, for all the reasons suggested earlier, such cases are few. One most illuminating example of judicial action that both resolved an environmental controversy directly and provides the opportunity for a detailed examination of the judicial function in coping with environmental evidence arose recently in New Jersey. Though—as is to be expected in an incipient legal area—the judge approached the problem rather indirectly through conventional legal doctrines, the case is nonetheless illuminating, and should set at rest most conventional fears about the ability of courts to inquire intelligently into the merits of environmental cases.

The case is Texas Eastern Transmission Company v. Wildlife Preserves, Inc.[1] and it arose in the following setting.

[1] 48 N.J. 261, 225 A.2d 130 (1966), 49 N.J. 403, 230 A.2d 505 (1967). Unlike most environmental cases, here the industry is the plaintiff and the environmental defenders are defendants. The reason is that the gas transmission company was seeking to take lands owned by Wildlife Preserves, and therefore the company had to initiate condemnation proceedings in court.

Wildlife Preserves, Incorporated, a private nonprofit organization, was in the business of acquiring important natural habitats for scientific study, aesthetic enjoyment, and wildlife maintenance. Among its holdings was Troy Meadows, a fourteen-hundred-acre tract in Morris County, New Jersey—"one of the finest inland fresh water marshes in the Northeast United States." Texas Eastern Transmission Corporation, a gas pipeline company, needed a right of way for a lateral extension from its main line south of Troy Meadows to a residential area to the north. Using its power of eminent domain, Texas Eastern sought to condemn a fifty-foot wide swath across the Meadows.

Troy Meadows was not the only possible route for the pipeline, but for reasons which have become familiar in many resource controversies, it was a likely choice. Undeveloped land is ordinarily cheaper, more convenient for construction and maintenance, and less disruptive to a wide range of human activities, and within or near urban areas there is little undeveloped land left except swamp, submerged lands, and parks. The very characteristics that make such areas attractive for developers and utilities at a late stage of urbanization make them battlegrounds for conservation interests—they are likely to be scarce, natural habitats within densely populated areas. Moreover, being in close proximity to established developments, they are not likely to be examples of pristine wilderness. From the developer's perspective, his proposal is only a modest extension of what is already essentially a *fait accompli*. To those who oppose further incursions, it is this very fact which poses the pervasive "nibbling" problem.

Troy Meadows fitted exactly within this conventional situation. It was circumscribed by busily traveled roads, abutted a residential housing development, and already contained two significant developments at the time Texas Eastern instituted its suit to condemn a right-of-way. Along the wooded upland part of the tract on its western side was a fifty-foot-wide cleared area under which lay the gas pipeline of another company, the so-called "Algonquin route"; to the east, in the marsh area, was an electric power right-of-way where overhead transmission lines were strung on high towers.

Texas Eastern originally sought to condemn its right-of-way in the wooded area, directly to the west of the Algonquin route; it desired to clear this area, bring in its heavy equipment to dig a trench, lay its pipe, and then cover the pipe with the earth it previously excavated.

Wildlife Preserves had three possible lines of defense against Texas Eastern: that the lateral pipeline was unnecessary, that it should avoid Wildlife Preserves' land, or that the route chosen on its land was not the least destructive of the alternatives available. It ultimately chose the last, and most modest, argument. The decision was clearly a tactical one and at least in one sense an extremely sound one, for it obtained a hearing and decision on the merits— in itself a considerable achievement.

The first question in the case was not whether Wildlife Preserves was correct in its assertion that it had a better route, but whether it had a legal right to litigate that question.[2] Under traditional legal doctrine, the answer would

[2] The case went straight to the Supreme Court for resolution of this legal question. The Supreme Court decided that Wildlife Preserves was entitled to a trial in which it could present its defense against the condemnation. The case was then remanded to the Superior Court so that a trial could be held on the propriety of Texas Eastern's condemnation plans.

have been a simple "no," for courts have usually deferred to the decisions of those who have eminent-domain power as they do to administrative agencies generally, on the assumption that their concept of the public interest is unassailable—leaving property owners only the opportunity to argue that they received an insufficient amount of money as compensation.

Only in one situation is the propriety of condemnation usually subject to challenge on the merits: if the owner of the condemned land can establish that his property is already devoted to a public purpose, the condemnor must prove that the proposed use is more in the public interest than the existing use. This, of course, is precisely the issue that citizens in many environmental cases want to litigate.

Traditionally, only publicly owned property such as parks or schools were treated as being devoted to a public use, and thus the question of the paramount public interest was permitted to be litigated only among contending public agencies.

The great achievement of the lawyer for Wildlife Preserves was that he was able to persuade the court that even privately owned land could be devoted to public use, and if so, its owners should be entitled to challenge the claim that the proposed new use would advance the public interest. Maintenance by a private organization of a natural habitat for the benefit of the general public, he successfully argued, was like a public use. In short, he persuaded the court to allow private citizens to defend the right to maintain a natural habitat as a part of the public trust belonging to the people.

The claim that operation of a wildlife preserve was an activity invested with a public interest, entitled to the same consideration at law, was cloaked in traditional legal terms; but it nudged the court to a position in which concern with preservation of the environment was put on a footing with the interest in its exploitation. The court decided that the public interest in maintenance of the preserve entitled its owner to a full trial "of its claim that a satisfactory alternate route is available to [Texas Eastern] which will not result in such irreparable damage to the preserve."

The Supreme Court then sent the case back to the Superior Court for a trial,[3] calling the attention of the trial judge to experts' affidavits filed by Wildlife Preserves that could be used to focus the issues and mold the case manageably for a decision. "These experts allege," the Supreme Court noted,

> that there is a sound alternate route for the pipeline to the east of [Texas Eastern's] proposed right-of-way . . . but still running over a portion of defendant's preserve. It is said also that this alternate way will serve [Texas Eastern's] purpose, and will avoid the important wooded areas entirely and nearly all trees. . . . Additional advantages to the preserve, as well as some physical and maintenance benefits which will inure to [Texas Eastern], are described.

With this framing of issues, responsive to the principal concerns of Wildlife Preserves but sharpened to make them amenable to a court's ordinary fact-finding capacities, the Supreme Court found a middle ground between unthinking deference to the supposed expertise of those with the power

[3] The remanded case is Texas Eastern Transmission Corp. v. Wildlife Preserves, Inc., Sup. Ct. N.J., Law Div., Morris Cty., Morristown, N.J., Docket No. L-13684-64 (Jan. 1967).

of eminent domain and the opening of a Pandora's box for every crank who is offended when a utility or a builder proposes operations in his neighborhood.

Nor was the court oblivious to the fact that excessive protraction of the proceedings might itself deny the very justice sought to be done. In remanding the case, it ordered that it be set down for immediate trial. Considering the degree of concern often expressed about the untoward delay engendered by judicial intervention, it is appropriate to note that a sensitive court *is* capable of flexibility and *can* expedite a case where circumstances demand it. In this particular matter, the Supreme Court decision was issued on December 5, 1966. The case went to trial in the Superior Court on January 9, 1967, and the judge issued his decision on January 19, 1967—a total lapse of forty-four days.

It would have been perfectly understandable if one had predicted that the trial ordered in the Wildlife Preserves case would turn out to be a legal disaster. For it was at the trial that the reasonable questions posed by the Supreme Court's opinion would have to be reduced to manageable, and comprehensible, facts and thus made amenable to an acceptable ruling of law. That would seem no easy task, as the choice between a route next to the existing Algonquin pipeline in the wooded upland and a route through the marsh involved a comparison of projected effects ranging over a wide spectrum of technical areas of scientific expertise: testimony would have to be given by experts on soils and erosion, botany, engineering, geology, ornithology, and ecology. And to provide whatever confirmation might be needed of the worst fears one might have, the judge announced at an early point in the trial: "I will advise you that . . . before this case started I looked up the meaning in the dictionary of ecology because I noted it in the Supreme Court's opinion. I was not aware of that before."

The witnesses for Wildlife Preserves testified first, as they had the initial burden of proof under the Supreme Court's order. Their case consisted of three elements: evidence as to the value and uniqueness of the land in question as a natural habitat; evidence as to the damage produced by the existing pipeline, it being assumed that the proposed pipeline would be constructed in a similar fashion and thus produce additional damage of a similar kind; and evidence as to the lesser harm to be anticipated if the pipeline were laid in the marshy area along the route of the existing electric transmission lines.

The trial was essentially an extended discourse on the process of laying an underground pipeline. Wildlife Preserves' witnesses focused on the principal stages of that process: the initial clearing of the area so that heavy equipment could be brought in and space made available to dig a trench and store excavated earth; the period of laying the pipeline when the route area was in a highly disturbed condition; and the period following construction when the soil over the pipeline would be relaid so as to provide easy maintenance.

The picture drawn by Wildlife Preserves' witnesses was one where a strip of land would be first cleared to open the way for excavation. In the process many old and large trees would be cut, thus reducing the already limited wooded habitat needed as an adjunct to the marsh ecosystem. Removal of trees that served as a wind shield would thereby further reduce the wooded area and spoil the area's appearance. The process of excavation itself, they testified, held many perils. The Algonquin pipeline experience had

had these effects—during the period when the trench for that pipeline was open and soil was piled high, there was a good deal of erosion into nearby waters. The effect was the washing of much sediment into one stream, a form of pollution leaving a permanent turbidity problem.

Moreover, they said, the construction itself would break stream banks and produce further erosion and sedimentation. The recovery of plant life in the excavated area was another serious problem. The process of digging a trench and then returning the soil haphazardly, without preserving the topsoil layer, would modify the previous pattern of plant life on the land; heavy equipment would break roots throughout the area; and there would be a problem of compaction of soil which would further impede regeneration of plant life.

By contrast, the witnesses indicated that the laying of a pipeline in the soft, marsh area would not produce such disruption initially, and it could be expected that the process of regeneration in the marsh would be more rapid and more consistent with previous conditions.

For a considerable time the judge listened quietly to this detailed and technical evidence. One did not have to read his mind to feel confident that he looked forward with no little apprehension to the prospect of having to pass on the comparative credibility of witnesses who might differ as to the degree of sedimentation to be expected from soil areas of different slopes or on the relative regenerative powers of various types of soil. Was the case really one which involved either deciding between contrasting views of differing schools of scientific thought and analysis, or about the amount of wooded upland required to sustain a given marsh? If so, it would be a difficult and unpleasant case indeed.

The judge gave the parties great latitude in introducing evidence and speaking their minds. He was obviously deeply interested—as well he might be, for he had the responsibility of making a decision—in finding out just exactly what points of conflict separated them. It is perhaps this attitude, or professional frame of reference, that particularly distinguishes the litigation process. It is relatively extravagant in the time it is willing to invest in letting interested persons state, be tested on, and restate their positions. It is intensive and attuned to detail and specificity— it has before it at a given moment only one particular controversy, and its decision must be responsive to the facts of this particular case. And, of course, it is pragmatic —the case must be decided; it cannot be left with a dozen loose ends and unresolved conflicts.

Because judges are routinely faced with litigation from the whole range of human enterprises that often involve details with which they are not familiar, it is quite common for them to feel their way around a case reaching for an answer to the question: What is really the common point of dispute in this controversy that transcends, for example, the complex day-to-day detail of running a railroad, a department store, or the stock market? It is the question which a professional decision-maker always asks the experts, assuming a certain commonality in conflict; and judges are preeminently professional decision-makers.

It was this attitude which Judge Joseph Stamler brought to the Wildlife Preserves case, and a reading of the transcript makes it clear that it was this common issue in the dispute that he was seeking out of the welter of detail. Fortunately, the Wildlife Preserves' witnesses gave him the answer to that question fairly early in the trial, and from that point the litigation began to take shape toward a decision. It became apparent as the testimony went forward that all the complaints about loss of tree cover, erosion, compaction, sedimentation, and so forth seemed to turn upon the claim that when a company came to lay a pipeline, they came to their task in a quite vigorous and unstinting fashion. It was obviously a process of "clear it all out, move the dirt fast and cheaply, lay it on and go forward to the next job."

Perhaps, then, it was not so much a question of the fact of a pipeline or of a particular location for it, but the manner in which a construction job was done and the degree of care that those construction techniques evidenced in the interests of preserving the remaining or preexisting uses of the land in which they were employed. If this were indeed the case, if this is what the objectors were really complaining about, it might be perfectly possible to effect an adequate resolution of the case by focusing upon the potential for modification in construction techniques used, though that was not the issue that had originally been framed by either of the parties.

This notion came to the judge rather early in the trial, and he persisted in pressing the issue until he obtained a satisfactory resolution. It is fascinating to see how the professional decision-maker thus shapes and molds a controversy. After listening to a full day of testimony, the judge began to interpose his own questions. Could not this dispute be resolved, he kept asking, if some arrangements could be made to assure that Texas Eastern's construction practices were modified to reduce the dangers of erosion and siltation?

This question set the stage for examination of the next witness, and, it seems fair to say, for the testimony that ultimately decided the case. Wildlife Preserves called a very impressive and knowledgeable witness, William A. Niering, professor of botany at Connecticut College and Director of the Connecticut Arboretum. Counsel began to ask him a set of questions plainly designed to be responsive to the inquiries earlier put by the judge. Niering responded by noting a number of possible techniques, such as reducing the time when raw soil lay in the open, covering it with mulch to prevent run-off, reducing disturbance of the soil, and preserving as much ground cover as was possible, that supported the judge's intuition that the essence of this case was not so much a choice between routes as it was a dissatisfaction with the precautions taken by the pipeline company in their construction operations. Obviously, if constraints could reasonably be imposed upon construction techniques that would meet the landowners' major objections and still let the company use the route it wanted, a satisfactory conclusion might be obtained without having to confront vague issues of relative values or complex disputes over soil or plant behavior.

Counsel's next question opened the way for the case's ultimate resolution. He asked Niering a conventional question: "What in your opinion would be the best route from an ecological standpoint for the plaintiff to construct its proposed pipeline and under what conditions?"

Instead of saying that it should be in the marsh, which is what one might have expected from the case as it had developed earlier, Niering picked up on the point of construction-with-minimum-disturbance. Thus he said that the best route would be along the existing Algonquin route, which would involve no new land clearing, but under conditions that would sharply minimize the disturbance, such as moderating the use of heavy equipment, and other such protective techniques.

As soon as Niering's direct examination ended, the judge again intervened with a question to him that, in retrospect, one can clearly identify as the critical point in the resolution of the case:

> Q: Do you feel that specific conditions can be laid down by a qualified person which would insure an equitable relationship between the ability to construct the line according to your first choice and do the least disturbing of the Algonquin line?
> A: I would like to say yes but I don't know enough about the equipment that is employed.
>
> •　•　•
>
> Q: Now, do you think if we had good ecologists and good engineers working upon such conditions as you propose, that these specific conditions could be laid down by them?
> A: From my experience in right-of-way management, yes. . . .

The cross-examination of Professor Niering by counsel for Texas Eastern essentially consisted of one long hypothetical question: Suppose, Niering was asked, that Texas Eastern agreed to undertake its construction under a whole set of agreed-upon conditions, such as reducing the width of the right-of-way, double-ditching so that top soil would be replaced as such, and preserving larger trees—in such a case, would the construction be "consistent with good conservation practice?"

Niering said that it would be, suggesting in addition a few other conditions that ought to be met. Texas Eastern indicated that they were prepared to comply with these requirements, and from that point it was clear that as far as Judge Stamler was concerned the trial was essentially over. The landowners had predicated their case primarily on the disturbance problem—siltation, cutting of stream banks, compaction of soil, revegetation—and Texas Eastern had gone very far to accommodate those concerns. As to reduction of the wooded area, they had agreed to narrow their right-of-way to as little as ten feet to save a particularly important woodland section and had agreed further not to cut any large trees, which seemed a major concession to the objection about woodland habitat and wind shield.

One could hardly blame the judge for feeling that he had produced a remarkably good accommodation. Whether well-resolved or not from a scientific standpoint, the case moved toward resolution as effectively as could be expected in a human decision-making process. The mind cannot simultaneously and continuously juggle a multitude of diverse considerations—it must narrow toward a focus on the essential, casting out lesser and less relevant considerations. Whether intuitively, as in the judicial process, or quantitatively, as in a more mechanized decisional setting where discrete weights are assigned various factors, the process will inexorably move toward resolution of the few, or single, factors deemed most important. The lawyer for Wildlife Preserves and his client themselves shaped the case in a certain fashion, and the judge inevitably responded to that formulation. Had they chosen to ignore disturbance issues and fought the cutting of a woodland swath as the central issue, they would have had a different case, and quite possibly a different result.

What is important in these observations is that the case developed as a reflection of the concerns that the interested parties themselves evinced. Citizens can hardly ask more of their governmental institutions than that they respond by making an effort to resolve the problems which those citizens themselves identify as critical.

Moreover, the decision here was responsive in a detailed and specific fashion; it got right down to the particulars—where, and how, and how much. It was not a vague and flabby response based on some abstract considerations of whether good or bad precedents were being set, whether some constituency would or would not be offended, or whether some legalistic rule of burden of proof was or was not met. Notably, as the case was decided, neither such abstractions as burden of proof nor arbitrariness appeared to be of much importance. The decision developed out of the facts—organically.

The preceding comments imply that the case was essentially concluded before Texas Eastern even began to put its witnesses on the stand, and so, in practical effect, it was. All that was left was the ascertainment of a few details to determine their consistency with the solution that the judge had in mind. One such question was whether it was practicable to put the Texas Eastern pipeline wholly within the existing Algonquin right-of-way; if so, Wildlife Preserves' last concern would be abated. But Texas Eastern introduced engineering testimony to the effect that safety and standard practice cautioned that a greater separation would be needed between the lines than such a proposal would allow. Wildlife Preserves was unable to controvert this testimony.

Last, the question of the potential for running the pipe through the marsh was raised, for it remained to determine whether, even with the conditions now promised by Texas Eastern, the marsh route would be preferable. But this potentially troublesome question never had to be faced, for Texas Eastern produced engineering testimony that to build in the marsh would require building a dike to carry construction equipment and that the dike itself would be likely to create serious siltation problems, disturbance of the previous marsh habitat, and difficulties in revegetation. Wildlife Preserves was unable to establish that a dike was unnecessary or to controvert the asserted ecological problems a dike would create, and the demands for the marsh route dissolved.

Judge Stamler formally extracted from Texas Eastern all the promises relating to construction practices referred to earlier and entered judgment allowing the condemnation along the narrowed upland route dependent on those conditions' being adhered to. Wildlife Preserves again appealed to the New Jersey Supreme Court, but the appeal was destined to failure. Judge Stamler's judgment was affirmed quickly, and without dissent.

Beyond responsiveness and detailed consideration, the Wildlife Preserves case is remarkable for another element not often associated with the judicial process—flexibility. Too frequently litigation is viewed as an enterprise in which lawyers, steeped in rigor and bound by precedent, encase a controversy in turgid and unrealistic doctrine; in this case, however, neither doctrine nor the preexisting expectations of the parties determined the result. A third alternative, promoted at first by neither litigant, became the basis for decision—an alternative that grew naturally out of the testimony as it developed. It is in a way ironic and amusing that the virtues of responsiveness to reality, flexibility, broader bases for choice, the search for alternatives—all the goals so much lauded by planners and thinkers in the resource field, but so rarely revealed in conventional decisional processes—should find realization in the one forum to which those experts have hardly ever turned, the judiciary.

Perhaps there is a lesson in this, taught by a local judge in Morristown, New Jersey, who had to look up the word "ecology" in the dictionary before he came into the courtroom. Perhaps judges, who have been doing so much deferring in the area of resource management, have earned a bit of deference for themselves.

Though the words were never used during the lawsuit, the Wildlife Preserves case was a clear example of the public trust doctrine at work.[4] The public values provided by the Wildlife Preserves tract would ordinarily be appropriable as a free good by a private enterpriser. While compensation would have to be paid for the underlying land taken, the lack of any ordinary means for marketing or evaluating the diffuse benefits of such land to the general public—as a base for wildlife from which many disparate and unidentifiable citizens benefit, to take but a single example—would usually mean that no money equiva-

[4] The case is a variant only in a technical sense. Instead of a government agency, the challenged party is a private company holding governmental power to condemn land; and the challenger, though in the formal position of a private landowner, sought to protect the interests of the public for whose benefit the tract was established and maintained.

lent would be provided for those losses.[5] Moreover, even if compensation were paid that was sufficient to buy equivalent land, the total stock of such lands could not be enlarged—if Wildlife Preserves were to take ownership of another tract, there would still be a net loss of the kind of habitat that comprised the preserve.

Under ordinary circumstances, then, the public values inherent in the Wildlife Preserves tract would have been taken without charge, just as clean air and water have been taken. The significance of the New Jersey case is that the court treated those public values as entitled to the same legal protection that any private property right demands. The neighboring property owner (here the pipeline company) was compelled to use its property as not to injure that of another (the beneficiaries of Wildlife Preserves). Every reasonable step had to be taken to minimize the losses to one user by the legitimate uses of another, as a workable alternative to compensation in money for anticipated losses. The Wildlife Preserves case is thus a specific, and successful, implementation of the principle *"sic utere tuo ut alienum non laedas."*

The judicial experiment carried out in the Wildlife Preserves case is readily adaptable to larger problems, such as the Alaska pipeline, strip-mining, highways, location of factories and power plants—to areas of conduct in which public resources—the public trust—are endangered. Where a reasonable accommodation can be worked out technically, the particular sort of remedy applied in the Wildlife

[5] In theory, such values could be determined and compensation in money made to citizens as beneficiaries of the trust. In practice, though, the law ignores or, at best, distinctly undervalues them.

Preserves case can be used. Where no such accommodation is possible, the court may have to thrust upon the legislature the burden of deciding whether, and to what extent, it is prepared to sacrifice existing public values to proposed new developments and what risks it ought to take in the absence of adequate protective technology.

In some situations, where public values are capable of replacement and where they can be evaluated in dollars, it may be appropriate to order compensation in dollars for the acquisition of substitute facilities. This approach has sometimes been used when parklands are taken for other purposes.[6] It is also possible to use the threat of subsequent liability for restoration work as a deterrent against operations that threaten public values; some modest steps in this direction have already been taken in respect to oil spills.[7] Similarly, operations such as strip-mining may be conditioned upon an obligation to expend the funds necessary to restore the land surface; this technique has also been tried.[8]

While these devices are appropriate subjects for legislation, they will not always be enacted adequately or in time. The presence of a common-law public trust doctrine—which recognizes public rights as entitled to enforcement—serves to deal with problems which have not been resolved by statute.

[6] See Joseph L. Sax: "The Public Trust Doctrine in Natural Resource Law," 68 Michigan Law Review at 471, 482 note 35 (1970).

[7] E.g., Water Quality Improvement Act of 1970, Public Law 91-224, 83 Stat. 91; Ch. 572, Public Laws of Maine (1970), Ch. 3, title 38, Maine Revised Statutes.

[8] U.S. Department of the Interior, *Surface Mining and Our Environment* (Washington, D.C., Government Printing Office, 1967).

Chapter 11

Nice
Sentiments
Are Not
Enough

Talking about the prospects for environmental litigation makes most people very uncomfortable. "A lawsuit over every marsh!" they ask. "We must do better than that."

We will do better, but not nearly so well as the public likes to think. We have many battles ahead that will have to be fought one by one. The battlefield, of course, will not be limited to the courtroom—many disputes will be aired in the legislative forum, before administrative tribunals, and in the mass media. But one fundamental source of power to make those battles productive will be the hovering presence of a court order.

This is not because courts are—in some theoretical sense —particularly desirable institutions for the resolution of conflicts; but because within the foreseeable future there will *be* conflicts and because courts are especially suitable for assuring access to the decision-making process to ordinary citizens who have no status beyond that as the victims of environmental disruption.

This fact does not imply elimination of the administrative process nor abandonment of large solutions in favor of perpetual incremental problem-solving. Rather it suggests the need to add to that process a dimension that incorporates citizen participation as one essential and continuing factor in the search for environmental quality.

Neither does recognition of the need for an enlarged judicial role cast doubt on the essential search for technological solutions or improved methods of economic measurement. It is often said, for example, that one fundamental problem is the existence of a market system which undervalues or ignores many of the costs of poor environmental management. A plant creating air pollution may provide immediate benefits in the form of jobs, tax revenues, and dividends to stockholders. Those benefits are easily visible. The costs to a diffuse population—diffuse both in time and space—in medical expenses, amenity values, and long-term health hazards may be even greater. Plainly, every effort should be made to devise systems for evaluating and incorporating in the planning process those costs and benefits that are now insufficiently taken into account.

Even if such a system were carefully fashioned, however, it would have to be applied to particular instances individually by an administrative tribunal subject to all the human and political pressures that we have seen operating in the preceding pages. The dubious applications of cost-benefit analysis by agencies like the Bureau of Reclamation and the Army Corps of Engineers should caution us against undue optimism about the values of theoretical solutions isolated from adequate enforcement mechanisms. It must never be forgotten that a solution that incorporates the public interest in a large sense may be extremely disadvantageous to particular groups or individuals whose interest or power is not dissipated by the mere existence of a rational scheme for planning and project evaluation. The man whose job is at stake or whose tract of land is subject to restraints for the greater good of the society will still sustain a personal loss that he may be unwilling to sacrifice to the larger benefit of his fellows.

Every large-scale proposal to promote greater concern for environmental quality has within it the potential for conflict that must ultimately be worked out at the individual level and may invite the interposition of concerned citizens. An effluent tax scheme, for example, that would largely replace the present enforcement scheme for water pollution control with a self-enforcing tax levied on discharges, would at some point lead to controversy over the assessment of charges upon individual water users. The desire to keep tax bills down is unlikely to disappear no matter how committed the society becomes to the goal of clean water.

It is, of course, true that the more rigorous a scheme becomes, the less the scope for potential controversy. A law prohibiting any parkland from being taken for highways will substantially limit dispute over that particular issue, but we cannot resolve the highway routing problem so neatly. And while we can purchase or set aside specific tracts of land as public wilderness or wetland preserves, no rule is going to be promulgated that will determine in advance where each new power plant or airport is to be located. The search for absolutes is alluring, but largely illusory. Few environmental problems are amenable to a fixed set of "thou-shalt-nots," and any attempt to transform the latter into governing rules only forces the real process of decision-making out of public sight and into the dark recesses of bureaucracy.

For a great many environmental issues, legislatures will never be able to do more than state large policy choices and encourage decision makers to broaden the perspectives on the basis of which individual decisions are made. The increasing breadth of a vision that legislatures are demanding in resource management is all to the good; yet, paradoxically, the broader the perspectives required, the less satisfactory the administrative agency appears as a final repository of policy-making. The need for judicial intervention will thus diminish only to the extent that relatively clear-cut and self-enforcing policy decisions can be articulated—a prospect that is likely for only a modest number of problems.

These observations are not intended to discourage the search for general solutions, but rather to indicate the large element of sentimentalism that tends to infect our thinking about environmental issues. Probably no aspect of the current public concern for the environment demonstrates this problem more openly than the pervasive desire for the enactment of a "conservation bill of rights." Proposals for this take various forms. One version recently introduced in the Congress declared that "the right of the people to clean air, pure water, freedom from excessive and unnecessary noise, and the natural scenic, historic and esthetic qualities of their environment shall not be abridged." Other proposals describe "an indefeasible interest in a liveable environment and an inalienable right to protect that interest" or the right to "an unimpaired physical environment." Some people even say that we already have constitutional protection for the environment in the form of the Ninth Amendment, which provides that the "enumeration in the Constitution, of certain rights, shall not be construed to deny or disparage others retained by the people."

Certainly, constitutional recognition of the right to a decent environment would betoken our good intentions and help to set before us a goal toward which our society ought to aspire. But it would be naïve to believe that any such declaration could be a substitute for the dreary task of dealing with the environmental problems that must be met and resolved daily in a thousand individual cases. In itself, a constitutional amendment would save not a single wetland or forest; it would remove no cement plants or automobile exhausts; and it would clean no streams.

Some say that a constitutional amendment "could do for the environment what the Fifth Amendment has done for civil rights." A slight emendation of this statement is required for accuracy's sake—it is what the Constitution *and the courts* have done that we recall with pride.

An essential question that must be asked whenever proposals for an environmental declaration of rights are raised is whether those rights are going to be enforceable, and if so, by whom. The value of moral pressure should not be ignored; but its importance in enforcing those rights depends to a great extent on the context in which the declaration is made. Fifty years ago—when it was widely thought that dumping odious industrial effluent into streams was an inalienable part of a landowner's property right—a declaration of the right of the people to clean air and water might have represented a dramatic step forward. Today, however, one would have to search far and wide to find anyone unwilling to endorse the sentiments of the constitutional amendment proposed to Congress and quoted above.

The difficulty is that such an amendment would have different *practical* implications for the timber company executive and for the wilderness enthusiast—which simply emphasizes the doubts one must have about its value. For one problem with environmental declarations of rights is that they lack the substantive content that surrounds constitutional provisions like those governing free speech or the free exercise of religion, which, for all their uncertainty, incorporate specific historical experiences that infuse meaning based on a common understanding within the community.

An environmental declaration of rights would lack this important advantage. If its purpose were to encourage administrative agencies to adopt the view that they have environmental responsibilities, the declaration would come late in the game—that was yesterday's battle. Even those agencies which are the favorite targets of conservationists now perceive themselves as having environmental responsibilities. The Corps of Engineers no longer says it is simply interested in the problems of navigation. Nor do highway departments claim to be solely interested in building roads—at the beginning of the New Jersey hearing on the proposed Interstate 95, discussed in Chapter 5, the state highway official began the proceedings with the following remarks:

> We have to take the rap whether it's good, bad or indifferent, but we have really studied and listened to some of the experts . . . on the matter of scenic beauty and wildlife and the historic values, etc., and in spite

of the fact that we're often considered a bunch of clam-diggers who only think about price and where an alignment is to go, we actually have some taste for esthetics as well. . . . I want you to know that long before the origin of beautification came out of Washington, that we had some taste other than in our mouth.

So long as an official *thinks* that he is thinking environmentally, a declaration is not likely to change things perceptibly. Today one would have to look very far indeed to find an official who did not agree with, and believe he was working to enforce, the ideals of "the right to a decent environment."

Today's problems begin with a challenge to administrators over what they are doing, not what they are saying. Enforcement is the battleground, as the discussion of the National Environmental Policy Act and the Alaska oil pipeline in Chapter 3 should have made eminently clear.

A final word about environmental declarations of rights and the Constitution is needed before leaving this subject. There is an important, and insufficiently understood, distinction between a declaration of the right to a decent environment appearing in a statute and one appearing in the Constitution. A right with constitutional status does indeed create the opportunity for its enforcement in the courts, but it also—and herein lies the danger—gives courts *ultimate* authority. That is, an environmental right declared by the courts as a matter of constitutional law cannot be overruled by the legislature. By contrast, a court enforcing a statutory right (even though it may have the same wording as a constitutional provision) can always be overruled by subsequent legislation.

This distinction has great implications, particularly in the light of American legal history. It is worth recalling here that in the pre-New Deal era a reactionary U.S. Supreme Court invalidated a good deal of important and needed legislation, thus provoking a grave constitutional crisis that abated only when one member of the Court finally changed his position—it was this event that produced the *bon mot*: "A switch in time saved Nine."

We ought not to re-create the potential for such crises, remote as they may seem today. A court—even with the best motive—should not be authorized to function as an environmental czar against the clear wishes of the public and its elected representatives.[1] It is not necessary to take such risks. Today both state and federal legislatures have the authority they need to protect the environment; except in rare instances, legislatures need no additional constitutional authority to enact environmental protection laws. A statutory declaration of rights can open environmental

---

[1] As the discussion of the public trust doctrine (Chapter 7) indicates, courts tend to view themselves as having some implicit constitutional powers that can be used to overrule legislative conduct utterly at odds with the public interest. So long as such authority is treated as very limited, to be used most sparingly, it is acceptable; but we should not promote general environmental rule-making by the courts under a constitutional imprimatur.

Certainly the Ninth Amendment to the U.S. Constitution need not necessarily be read as creating a constitutional right to a decent environment. A detailed analysis of this much-discussed provision must be left to the exigetical skills of constitutional lawyers. Suffice it to say here that the Amendment is a vessel into which one can pour pretty much whatever he wants. It is no more obviously applicable to a decent environment than it is to some purported right to be paid in gold coin, to have adequate medical treatment, or to be free of chlorinated drinking water. The merits of such claims are not advanced by reciting the Ninth Amendment over them. In all probability, the provision was the Founding Fathers' elegant way of expressing the hope that they had not forgotten anything important in the Bill of Rights.

matters fully to judicial attention but still leave ultimate decision-making power in the hands of the elected representatives of the public.

While the theme of this book has been a plea for greater judicial intervention, it should be eminently clear that our goal is to create *additional* leverage for the citizen— to add to, not diminish, the opportunities for redress; to improve and provoke the democratic process, not to constrain it. Courts are powerful enough so long as they are enabled to build a common law for the environment, remand dubious proposals to the legislatures, and declare moratoria.

Moreover, there is a fundamental difference between almost all environmental problems and the issues to which the bill of rights, so often used as an analogy, is addressed. Essentially, the bill of rights deals with the problems of permanent minorities and with government oppression of unpopular individuals or groups. For such problems, where the danger is tyranny by the majority, some foil is needed to the majoritarian rule that governs the legislative process. Giving ultimate, constitutional authority to the courts in the matter of free speech and the rights of the criminal defendant or the religious dissenter is most appropriate. But environmental questions are pre-eminently problems caused by powerful and well-organized minorities who have managed to manipulate governmental agencies to their own ends. For such issues, the need is for a forum that can help to even the political and administrative leverage of the adversaries; if that equalization *per se* can be accomplished judicially, the courts may then properly withdraw and leave the ultimate decision to a truly democratized democratic process.

Conclusion

Ultimately, the question we must ask ourselves is whether we are prepared to leave the public interest to hired hands. In 1967, shortly before the decision was made to lease federal submerged lands off Santa Barbara, California, for oil and gas production, a meeting was held in the office of the Under Secretary of the Interior. Present were not only the government officials directly involved with mineral production, but also representatives of those bureaus and offices concerned with the whole range of environmental quality problems. The Under Secretary went around the room, asking each man whether there was any objection from the perspective of those values with which his agency was concerned. Not a single objection was raised. In that event, the Under Secretary is reported to have said, there was no basis for preventing production from going forward.

The decision, now inscribed in oil on Santa Barbara's beaches, was later described by former Secretary of the Interior Stewart Udall as "a sort of conservation Bay of Pigs."[1] Yes. But what could the poor Secretary do? The Budget Bureau, he testified, was "hungry for revenue," and "a Presidential decision had been made about getting

[1] "Hearings Before the Subcommittee on Air and Water Pollution, Senate Committee on Public Works, Water Pollution—1969," part 4, p. 1280 (91st Cong., 1st Sess.); see also parts 2 and 3.

more money to help balance the national budget. . . . Communications from the Budget Bureau were indicating to us that we should have a maximum leasing program."

Only the nonexperts, the residents of Santa Barbara, were dubious. When questions were raised, federal officials responded publicly with a letter which said: "[We] feel maximum provision has been made for the local environment and that further delay in lease sale would not be consistent with the national interest." Privately, though, an interagency memorandum was circulated commenting that "the 'heat' has not died down but we can keep trying to alleviate the fears of the people," and noting that pressures were being applied on the agencies by the oil companies whose equipment, "costing millions of dollars," was being held "in anticipation."

The story was succinctly told in a memorandum written by the Interior Department's staff engineer after a meeting with officials from the Army Corps of Engineers—Interior was unhappy that the Corps had decided to hold a public hearing at Santa Barbara. The memo reported as follows:

> Discussion centered around "public interest" aspects in our offshore operation. Outlined what we had done and how it appeared to conflict with the Corps public hearing. . . . Of course how they handled the public was their business, but we did not have to participate. . . . I pointed out that we . . . had tried to warn the L.A. Dist. Engineer of what he faced and we preferred not to stir the natives up any more than possible. . . .

Ultimately, of course, the "natives" at Santa Barbara did get stirred up, when their oil-blackened beaches demonstrated the efficiency of those "maximum provisions"

that had been made for the local environment. A Santa
Barbara county supervisor later recalled:

> You may ask why we at the local level didn't stress spill-
> age controls. The answer is simple. It was discussed
> many times, but always Interior Department and oil
> industry officials led us to believe we had nothing to
> fear. They said they had perfected shutoff devices that
> were foolproof even in such disasters as a ship running
> into the platform, or an earthquake.

A Santa Barbara business executive summed up the
mood of citizens who have dealt with our official guardians
of the environment:

> We are so goddamned frustrated. The whole democratic
> process seems to be falling apart. Nobody responds to
> us, and we end up doing things progressively less reason-
> able. This town is going to blow up if there isn't some
> reasonable attitude expressed by the federal government.
> Nothing seems to happen except that we lose.

But government is beginning to respond. The voice of
the citizen is beginning to be heard, and an answer to his
plea is emerging. While still sitting on the U.S. Court of
Appeals, Judge Warren Burger, the present Chief Justice
of the United States, had before him a case in which private citizens sought to challenge the grant of a license by
the Federal Communications Commission.[2] The Commission had excluded them on the ground that *it* was there to
protect the public interest and needed no help from citizen busybodies. To this Judge Burger responded:

2 Office of Communication of the United Church of Christ v. Federal
Communications Commission, 359 F.2d 994 (D.C. Cir. 1966), 425 F.2d
543 (D.C. Cir. 1969).

The theory that the Commission can always effectively represent the [public] interests . . . without the aid and participation of legitimate [citizen] representatives fulfilling the role of private attorneys general is one of those assumptions we collectively try to work with so long as they are reasonably adequate. When it becomes clear, as it does to us now, that it is no longer a valid assumption which stands up under the realities of actual experience, neither we nor the Commission can continue to rely on it.

. . .

We cannot fail to note that the long history of complaints . . . had left the Commission virtually unmoved . . . and it seems not unlikely that the . . . application might well have been routinely granted except for the determined and sustained efforts of [citizen] Appellants at no small expense to themselves.

Despite the sharpness of his language, Judge Burger, as a good traditionalist, decided to give the Commission another opportunity to do its duty. The case was sent back to the agency for further proceedings, in which the Commission imposed upon the citizen intervenors an impossibly heavy burden of proof as well as declaring most of their arduously acquired evidence inadmissible. Again it ruled that the license should be issued. And again the case came to the court. This time, Judge Burger was left in no doubt about the implications of the insider perspective, and he ruled:

The record now before us leaves us with a profound concern over the entire handling of this case following the remand to the Commission. The impatience with the Public Intervenors, the hostility toward their efforts to satisfy a surprisingly strict standard of proof, plain errors in rulings and findings lead us, albeit reluctantly, to the conclusion that it will serve no useful purpose to ask the Commission to reconsider the . . . decision . . . The administrative conduct reflected in this record is beyond repair.

The Chief Justice is not much inclined toward grandiloquence, but he that day sounded the theme that will reverberate as a battle cry. "Consumers," he concluded laconically, "are generally among the best vindicators of the public interest."

Postscript

This has been a book about the game of government and how it is played to the detriment of the ordinary citizen. Everything that has been said here is adaptable to the problems of housing and welfare, to the proliferation of shoddy merchandise, and the miserable charade that too frequently passes for public regulation of business and the professions.

Environmental problems simply illustrate our failings with special poignancy: because we have left them unnoticed and unattended so long; because the ecologic quality of natural systems so strikingly attests the dangers of single-minded cutting, dredging, and damming; and, ironically, because environmental disruption affects the rich and powerful just as it does the most humble citizen. The plunder of our natural heritage at last brings home to us our equality—we all must breathe the same foul vapors. The well-to-do are not accustomed to being so dealt with; their frustration is now a seed that will bloom in many gardens.

Appendix:
A Model Law

The following law, drafted in its original form by the author, was introduced by Representative Thomas Anderson in the Michigan Legislature on April 1, 1969.[1] Its purpose is to make clear the authority of courts to take jurisdiction of the sort of litigation discussed in this book. While many courts have already undertaken consideration of such cases, the present role of the judiciary is uncertain, haphazard, and fragmentary. In some states judicial review of much administrative agency action is unavailable; if available at all, its scope is often very narrow, or there may be serious doubts about the "standing to sue" of private citizens who lack conventional economic interests. Sometimes there is no easily perceived legal duty that can be said to be violated, for the right of the public to a decent environment is now nowhere generally recognized in the law. Thus, as we have seen in cases such as the Hudson River Expressway dispute, courts may reach out for obscure statutory authority or may dismiss meritorious claims. This situation should

[1] The law was enacted in Michigan on July 27, 1970. Enrolled House Bill No. 3055, State of Michigan, 75th Legislative, Regular Session of 1970, Public Act No. 127 of 1970. A bill modeled after the Michigan law was introduced in the U.S. Senate (S. 3575, Senators Philip Hart and George McGovern) and in the House of Representatives (H.R. 16436, Representative Morris Udall) on March 10, 1970. At the time of this writing, similar bills had also been introduced in a number of other states, including New York, Massachusetts, Colorado, Pennsylvania, and Tennessee.

not be allowed to prevail. It is confusing and unfair both to courts and to litigants.

House Bill No. 3055 is an attempt to remedy this sorry situation. Its purposes are essentially threefold: to recognize the public right to a decent environment as an enforceable legal right; to make it enforceable by private citizens suing as members of the public; and to set the stage for the development of a common law of environmental quality. As to the last consideration, the bill purposely refrains from defining pollution, environmental quality, or the public trust. At this early stage in the development of environmental law it is important to open the way to elucidation and consideration of a wide range of problems, many of which are still uncertain, rather than to create confining definitions. Use of the courts to evolve a common-law approach to environmental problems adds to the arsenal of the public interest a significant weapon: the ability to meet problems as they are identified and to formulate a solution appropriate to the occasion—flexible, innovative, and responsive.

To open the way for common-law litigation is not to displace the legislative function in setting standards or defining in a precise fashion environmental rights and wrongs. Problems recognized and information elicited through litigation will promote and complement continuing and essential legislative action.

Moreover, as the bill makes clear, judicial action is not intended to supplant administrative regulation; it is, rather, meant to provide some needed review of the administrative process and a judicial forum in those inevitable instances where other regulatory processes are lacking or insufficient.

STATE OF MICHIGAN
75th LEGISLATURE
REGULAR SESSION OF 1970

Introduced by Rep. Thomas J. Anderson

ENROLLED HOUSE BILL No. 3055

AN ACT to provide for actions for declaratory and equitable relief for protection of the air, water and other natural resources and the public trust therein; to prescribe the rights, duties and functions of the attorney general, any political subdivision of the state, any instrumentality or agency of the state or of a political subdivision thereof, any person, partnership, corporation, association, organization or other legal entity; and to provide for judicial proceedings relative thereto.

The People of the State of Michigan enact:

Sec. 1. This act, shall be known and may be cited as the "Thomas J. Anderson, Gordon Rockwell environmental protection act of 1970".

Sec. 2. (1) The attorney general, any political subdivision of the state, any instrumentality or agency of the state or of a political subdivision thereof, any person, partnership, corporation, association, organization or other legal entity may maintain an action in the circuit court having jurisdiction where the alleged violation occurred or is likely to occur for declaratory and equitable relief against the state, any political subdivision thereof, any instrumentality or agency of the state or of a political subdivision thereof, any person, partnership, corporation, association, organization or other legal entity for the protection of the air, water and other natural resources and the public trust therein from pollution, impairment or destruction.

(2) In granting relief provided by subsection (1) where there is involved a standard for pollution or for an anti-pollution device or procedure, fixed by rule or otherwise, by an instrumentality or agency of the state or a political subdivision thereof, the court may:

(a) Determine the validity, applicability and reasonableness of the standard.

(b) When a court finds a standard to be deficient, direct the adoption of a standard approved and specified by the court.

Sec. 2a. If the court has reasonable ground to doubt the solvency of the plaintiff or the plaintiff's ability to pay any cost or judgment which might be rendered against him in an action brought under this act the court may order the plaintiff to post a surety bond or cash not to exceed $500.00.

Sec. 3. (1) When the plaintiff in the action has made a prima facie showing that the conduct of the defendant has, or is likely to pollute, impair or destroy the air, water or other natural resources or the public trust therein, the defendant may rebut the prima facie showing by the submission of evidence to the contrary. The defendant may also show, by way of an affirmative defense, that there is no feasible and prudent alternative to defendant's conduct and that such conduct is consistent with the promotion of the public health, safety and welfare in light of the state's paramount concern for the protection of its natural resources from pollution, impairment or destruction. Except as to the affirmative defense, the principles of burden of proof and weight of the evidence generally applicable in civil actions in the circuit courts shall apply to actions brought under this act.

(2) The court may appoint a master or referee, who shall be a disinterested person and technically qualified, to take testimony and make a record and a report of his findings to the court in the action.

(3) Costs may be apportioned to the parties if the interests of justice require.

Sec. 4 (1) The court may grant temporary and permanent equitable relief, or may impose conditions on the defendant that are required to protect the air, water and other natural resources or the public trust therein from pollution, impairment or destruction.

(2) If administrative, licensing or other proceedings are required or available to determine the legality of the defendant's conduct, the court may remit the parties to such proceedings, which proceedings shall be conducted in accordance with and subject to the provisions of Act No. 306 of the Public Acts of 1969, being sections 24.201 to 24.313 of the Compiled Laws of 1948. In so remitting the court may grant temporary equitable relief where necessary for the protection of the air, water and other natural resources or the public trust therein from pollution, impairment or destruction. In so remitting the court shall retain jurisdiction of the action pending completion thereof for the purpose of determining whether adequate protection from pollution, impairment or destruction has been afforded.

(3) Upon completion of such proceedings, the court shall adjudicate the impact of the defendant's conduct on the air, water or other natural resources and on the public trust therein in accordance with this act. In such adjudication the court may order that additional evidence be taken to the extent necessary to protect the rights recognized in this act.

(4) Where, as to any administrative, licensing or other proceeding, judicial review thereof is available, notwithstanding the provisions to the contrary of Act No. 306 of the Public Acts of 1969, pertaining to judicial review, the court originally taking jurisdiction shall maintain jurisdiction for purposes of judicial review.

Sec. 5. (1) Whenever administrative, licensing or other proceedings, and judicial review thereof are available by law, the agency or the court may permit the attorney general, any political subdivision of the state, any instrumentality or agency of the state or of a political subdivision thereof, any person, partnership, corporation, association, organization or other legal entity to intervene as a party on the filing of a pleading asserting that the proceeding or action for judicial review involves conduct which has, or which is likely to have, the effect of polluting, impairing or destroying the air, water or other natural resources or the public trust therein.

(2)   In any such administrative, licensing or other proceedings, and in any judicial review thereof, any alleged pollution, impairment or destruction of the air, water or other natural resources or the public trust therein, shall be determined, and no conduct shall be authorized or approved which does, or is likely to have such effect so long as there is a feasible and prudent alternative consistent with the reasonable requirements of the public health, safety and welfare.

(3)   The doctrines of collateral estoppel and res judicata may be applied by the court to prevent multiplicity of suits.

Sec. 6.   This act shall be supplementary to existing administrative and regulatory procedures provided by law.

Sec. 7.   This act shall take effect October 1, 1970.

This act is ordered to take immediate effect.

Index

access to decision-making process, 57, 100–7, 111–12, 202–5
administrative agencies:
  perspective of, 53–62, 83, 102; reform of, 63–107, deference to, 123–4, 181, 216
airports, 88–9
Alaska oil pipeline, 93–100, 118–19, 136
Aldrich, Alexander, 75, 76
Alexandria (Virginia) *Gazette*, 3, 7, 11
Anderson, Thomas J., 247, 249
arbitration, 84–107
Ashwaubenon v. Public Service Comm'n. (Wis.), 123

BASF Corp., Hilton Head Fishing Cooperative v. (S.C.), 103
Bayh, Birch, 18, 35–43
Beggs, James M., 84, 85
bill of rights, 234–9; *see also* litigation, public rights
Black, David S., 24–50, 53, 110
Bregman, Stanley, 42
Breitenstein, Jean S., 208
Bridwell, Lowell K., 87
Broyhill, Joel T., 7, 8
burden of proof, 176, 201–5
Bureau of Public Roads, 52
Burger, Warren E., 134, 242–4

Cabot, Lawrence, 75
Cain, Stanley A., 12–50, 52, 54, 71, 110
Cayuga Lake nuclear plant, 105

"Chaos or Uniformity in Boating Regulations?" (Cutler), 170
Chilson, Hatfield, 207, 208
Christian Science Monitor, 85, 86
Citizens' Committee for the Hudson Valley v. Volpe, (N.Y.), 128
Citizens' Committee on Natural Resources, 102
citizen participation, 57, 60, 100–7, 110–11, 232, 243
Citizens' Planning and Housing Association, 86
Cohen, Bernard, 44
common law approach, 162, 211, 230, 248
condemnation, 213–230; *see also* litigation
Connelly, Vaughn, 3
conservation bill of rights, 234–9; *see also* litigation, public rights
Consolidated Edison Co., 131
constitutional law: *see* litigation, public rights
Council on Environmental Quality (U.S.), 91–100
courts: role of, 108–24; competence of, 149–57; *see also* litigation
Crafts, Edward, 76
Cutler, Richard W., 170

d'Alesandro, Thomas, 87
decent environment, as a right: *see* public rights

Defenders of Florissant, Inc. v. Park Land Co. (Colo.), 207
delay, in litigation, 115–20, 207, 218
democratic theory, 58–60, 112, 152, 175–92, 196–9
Design With Nature (McHarg), 144
Dewey, Thomas E., 18, 19
Dingell, John, 13, 16, 23, 35–7, 66–7, 70–1, 77
Doyle, William E., 200–1
Dunham, A., 170
DuVal, Clive, 8

Eagles Nest Wilderness Committee, 195
effluent charges, 121
electric power, 114–15, 117, 131
eminent domain, 213–30
energy, 114–15, 117, 131, 213–30; *see also* Alaska oil pipeline
Environmental Defense Fund, xii
Environmental Defense Fund v. Corps of Engineers (Fla.), 210
Environmental Protection Act (Mich.), 249–52
Environmental Quality Council (U.S.), 91–100, 109
environmental rights: *see* public rights
estuarine protection, 55, 103, 186–9
Everglades, 21, 88–9, 105, 111
expertise, 60–2, 109–10, 141, 146–7, 149–57, 198–9, 212–30
externalities, 159–62, 172

Fairfax County Fed. of Citizens Assn's. v. Hunting Towers (Va.), 44
Favre, George, 85, 86
Federal Communications Commission, 134, 242
Federal Highway Administrator, 87, 101
Federal Power Commission, 107, 131–4
Field and Stream magazine, 20
Fish and Wildlife Coordination Act (U.S.), 65, 67
Florissant fossil beds, 206–8
free goods, 58–9, 229
Freedom of Information Act, 104
frivolous lawsuits, 115–20
Frome, Mike, 20, 21, 22, 45, 47
Future of San Francisco Bay, The (Scott, M.), 172

Galland, Marion, 6, 7, 8
Gandt v. Hardin (Mich.), 137–8, 209
Glasgow, Leslie L., 51, 66–72
Gottschalk, John S., 9–49, 53, 54, 88
Gould v. Greylock Reservation Commission (Mass.), 166, 184–6, 189–90
Grossman, Sanford, 18

H. P. Hoffman Associates v. Stanley R. Resor (D.C.), 51
Hall, R. G., 164
Harrison, Albertis S., 7
Hart, George L., Jr., 99
Hart, Philip A., xiii, 247
Hartzog, George B., Jr., 22, 49
hearings: *see* public hearings

Hickel, Walter J., 49, 50, 51, 53, 97, 99
Highway Route Selection Method (McHarg), 144
highways, 85–7, 114; Hudson River Expressway, 64–82, 101, 127–30, 133, 135–6, 147, 153–4; Alaska, 93–100; hearings on, 101–2; New Jersey, 138–48, 151–3; Massachusetts, 176–86
Hilton Head Fishing Cooperative v. BASF Corp. (S.C.), 103
Hoffman, Howard P., 5, 17, 18, 41, 42, 50
Holland, Ed, 42
Hopewell Township v. Goldberg (N.J.), 138
Hudson River Expressway, 64–82, 101, 108, 110, 127–30, 133, 135–6, 147, 156, 247
Hudson River Valley Commission, 65, 75, 83
Hughes, Bert, 76
Hughes v. Blair (N.J.), 189
Humelsine, Carlisle, 45, 46, 47
Hunting Creek, Virginia, 3–62, 70–3, 88, 110, 133, 156, 190, 202
Hunting Towers, 3, 17, 19
Hunting Towers Operating Company, 4, 17

Illinois Central Railroad v. Illinois (U.S.), 170
impeding environmental control, by litigation, 122–4
incremental decision-making, 53–6
independent agencies, 106–7; *see also* reform
insider perspective, 53–62, 83, 102, 109, 110, 243

institutional arrangements, 56–62
investigation, adequacy of, 65–100
Izaak Walton League, 44

Jackson, Henry M., 37, 39
Jones, Robert E., 33
judicial competence, 149–57; *see also* courts, litigation

Karth, Joseph E., 71
Keefe, Robert, 40, 41, 42
Keeley, John, 104
Kent, W. Wallace, 137, 209
Kimball v. MacPherson (Cal.), 171

Lee, R. W., 164
Life Magazine, 103
litigation: function of, 57, 108–24; crank suits, 115–20; preventive, 115–21; two-edged sword, 122–4; undermining regulation, 122–4; scope of traditional, 125–48; competence of courts, 149–57; planning, relation to, 154–5, 228; legislative function, relation to, 155–7, 163, 176, 231; public trust, 158–74; common law approach, 162; constitutional law, 170–1, 188–9; remands to legislature, 175–92; effectiveness, 180–92; publicity arising from, 189–90; measure of seriousness, 190–2; moratorium, 193–211; standing to sue, 196–7; separation of powers, 206; eminent domain, 213–30

Madison v. State (Wis.), 168
Madison v. Tolzman (Wis.), 170
market forces: *see* price, of environment
McCloskey, Paul N., Jr., 37, 38
McCormack, Edward, 42
McCormack, John W., 11, 12
McGovern, George, xiii, 247
McHarg, Ian, 139, 143–6
mediation, 84–107
Meyer, Bernie, 34
Michigan Environmental Protection Act, 249–52
Milwaukee v. State (Wis.), 167, 168
Moses, Robert, 104
Moses on the Green (Keeley), 104
Moss, John E., 10, 14, 15, 30, 31, 33, 38
Mowbray, A. Q., 75
Murphy, Thomas, 128, 129, 130

National Environmental Policy Act, 91–100
New York Times, The, 88
nibbling phenomenon, 22, 55, 214
Niering, William A., 223–5
Ninth Amendment, 234–9
Nixon, Richard M., 48, 85, 91–2
Northwest Ordinance, 164
nuclear power plants, 84, 105
nuisance law, 159–60

Office of Communication, United Church of Christ v. Federal Communications Commission (D.C.), 134, 242
Office of Environmental Quality (U.S.), 92

oil: development, 93–100; spills, 103, 150, 230, 240–2
ombudsman, 64, 82, 84–9
open-space preservation, 170, 213–30
Otten, Alan L., 84, 85
Ottinger, Richard, 80
Owings, Nathanial, 86–7, 88

Pankowski, Ted, 44
Parker v. United States (Colo.), 195–205, 209
parks, 176–86
Parks v. Simpson (Miss.), 186
People ex rel San Francisco Bay C. & D. v. Town of Emeryville (Cal.), 169
planning: organizations, 89–100; early review, 100–7; relation to litigation, 113–20; courts' effect on, 154–5, 228
Pocantico Hills, 73
Potomac River, 3–51
Pozen, Bill, 34, 35
Preservation of Open Space Areas (Dunham), 170
price, of environment, 58–9, 161–2, 172–3, 228–30, 232
Priewe v. Wisconsin State Land and Imp. Co. (Wis.), 171
private property, 58–60, 122–4, 158–60, 165, 173, 206–8, 229, 235
privileged information: *see* secrecy
procedures, burdensome, 105–6
public hearings, 101–2, 105–6
public ownership: *see* public rights

public participation, 57, 60,
100–7, 110–11, 232
public resources: *see* public
rights
public rights, 4, 58–60, 112,
123, 135, 147–8, 158–92, 196,
211, 216–17, 228–30, 234–9
public trust, 4, 158–74, 193–4,
211, 216, 228–30
Public Trust Doctrine, The
(Sax), 169, 230

racial discrimination, 17, 19
reform, 63–107
Reuss, Henry S., 10–51, 54
Rice, Harry, 76–81
right to a decent environment:
see public rights
riparian rights, 5, 12, 41
ripeness for review, 101, 103
*Rise and Evaporation of the
Mount Greylock Tramway*
(Tague), 184, 189–90
Rivers and Harbors Act (U.S.),
127, 128, 129, 130, 156
Road Review League v. Boyd
(N.Y.), 137
Road to Ruin (Mowbray), 75
Robbins v. Dept. of Public
Works (Mass.), 178
Rockefeller, Laurence 73, 80
Rockefeller, Nelson A., 73–83
Rockefeller Follies (Rodgers),
75
Rodgers, William, 75

Sacco v. Dept. of Public Works
(Mass.), 177
San Francisco Bay, 169–72
Santa Barbara, Cal., 103,
150, 240–2

Save San Francisco Bay Ass'n.
v. City of Albany (Cal.), 169
Saylor, John P., 10, 38, 99
Sax, Joseph L., 169, 230
Scenic Hudson Preservation
Conference v. Federal Power
Commission (N.Y.), 131–4,
135
Schwartz, John, 18, 40
Scott, M., 172
secrecy, 92, 102–4
separation of powers, 206
sic utere . . . , 158–60, 173,
229
Sierra Club, 195
Skidmore, Owings and Merrill,
86
Smith, Spencer, 102
Southern Living magazine, 21
sovereign immunity, xi
Sperling, Mike, 40, 41
spillover effects, 159–62, 172
Stamler, Joseph, 221, 225, 227
standing to sue, 125, 196–7, 247
State v. Public Service Comm'n.
(Wis.), 168
study, adequacy of, 65–100
study commissions, 84–107
sub-optimizing, 53, 110
supersonic transport, 84, 93
*Surface Mining and Our
Environment* (U.S. Department of the Interior), 230
Sutherland, Marvin, 47

Tague, William, 184, 189–90
task force, 84–100
Taylor v. Underhill (Cal.), 171
Teamsters' Union, 3
Teamsters' Union Pension
Fund, 4, 18

Texas Eastern Transmission Co. v. Wildlife Preserves (N.J.), 213–30
Texas Oyster Growers' Assoc. v. Odom (Tex.), 186
Thomson, James, 5, 6, 8
Township of Hopewell v. Goldberg (N.J.), 138
Train, Russell E., 49, 93–4
transportation: *see* highways, airports

Udall, Morris, xiii, 247
Udall, Stewart L., 7, 10, 21, 35, 49, 53, 73–82, 110, 240
U. S. Army Corps of Engineers, 4–51, 52, 65, 77, 81–2, 105–6, 128, 188, 209–10, 232, 236, 241
U. S. Department of Agriculture, 193–201
U. S. Department of the Interior, 7–51, 53–4, 65–82, 96–100, 119, 230, 232, 241–2

U. S. Department of Transportation, 65, 84
U. S. Forest Service, 137–8, 193–201

Vander Jagt, Guy, 25, 26, 35
Verkler, Jerry, 37

Wallace, McHarg, Roberts & Todd, 144
Wall Street Journal, 84, 105
Ward v. Mulford (Cal.), 171
Washington *Post*, 45, 88
waste reclamation, 121
Water Quality Improvement Act (U.S.), 230
Watt, Jim, 49
Wilderness Act (U.S.), 156, 157, 193–201, 209
Wilderness Society v. Hickel (D.C.), 99
Wildlife Preserves, Inc., 213–30

Yannacone, Victor, 208

A Note About the Author

Joseph L. Sax was born in Chicago in 1936. He received his B.A. from Harvard in 1957, and his J.D. from the University of Chicago in 1959. He is currently Professor of Law at the University of Michigan, and generally acknowledged as the nation's foremost expert on environmental law. He is a member of the Legal Advisory Committee to the President's Council on Environmental Quality, chairman of the American Bar Association's Committee on Public Lands and Waters, member of the ABA's Special Committee on Environmental Law, Trustee of the Center for Law and Social Policy in Washington, D.C., and chairman of the Editorial Advisory Board of the *Environmental Law Reporter*. He lives in Ann Arbor with his wife, Eleanor, and their three children.

A Note on the Type

The text of this book was set on the Linotype in a type face called Baskerville. The face is a facsimile reproduction of types cast from molds made for John Baskerville (1706-75) from his designs. The punches for the revived Linotype Baskerville were cut under the supervision of the English printer George W. Jones. John Baskerville's original face was one of the forerunners of the type style known as "modern face" to printers—a "modern" of the period A.D. 1800.

Typography and binding design by Virginia Tan